NANCY L. STIMSON

Searching
for
Shade

Jackie Smith

To order additional copies of this book, contact:
Xlibris
844-714-8691
www.Xlibris.com
Orders@Xlibris.com

Library of Congress Control Number: 2022914279
ISBN: Softcover   978-1-6698-4012-1
         Hardcover   978-1-6698-4013-8
         EBook   978-1-6698-4011-4

Print information available on the last page

Rev. date: 08/26/2022

Contents

Introduction

It took a while for me to realize that we could have died there. The only shade was the small shadow from my motorcycle that I could squeeze into by sitting on the running board. There is not a tree in sight anywhere. Just dry, barren desert and a cloudless sky.

It's 114 degrees with full sun, just outside of Peoria, Arizona. Fading fast, I am hot, light headed and feel like fainting, all in a matter of less than five minutes. It all began with my riding buddy Jackie, stopping to pour her drinking water over her burning thighs and head. We only rode another five miles and she was starting into heat exhaustion. Pulled off immediately onto a side road, desperate for shade, but not a single tree or building in sight. The temperatures in Arizona are the highest that either of us have ever experienced, we clearly did not realize how treacherous it could be.

We should have been in Alaska by now. A year ago, we started planning to ride to Alaska in July of 2021. Today we should be riding comfortably in jeans and a jacket in 60's and 70 degrees and 19 hours of daylight. Instead, we are dying of heat exhaustion on the edge of a dessert in 114 degrees. Covid 19 did us in. The borders remained closed. Could not enter Canada to get to Alaska, so we are traveling southwest instead.

This story is the actual trip itself, day by day, starting on July 1, 2021. It is about our search for shade during a global warming crisis, including high heat in New Mexico, Arizona, Nevada, California and South Dakota, and out of control fires burning thousands of acres in Arizona, Nevada, California and Oregon. It is about riding through smoke for hours blowing down from Manitoba across northern Minnesota, causing me to arrive home with respiratory and sinus issues, requiring weeks of medication.

The bright pink clusters of Fireweed in the burned forest of Yellowstone National Park remains the image of hope and renewed growth amid the devastation, like laughter, in the 8000 miles that we experienced together on our venture across this country we call home.

1

The Back Story

I grew up in rural Michigan as the second of five kids. We had mini bikes, dirt bikes and snowmobiles. My first motorcycle, a red 175 Yamaha, I proudly bought when I was about 19 or 20. I learned to love highway riding on this bike, rode it everywhere, including to work. My second motorcycle was a real gem, a 1982 Honda 400, dark red with red and pink pinstriping. I had a white faring and red saddle bags put on, and I rode that beauty all over Michigan, the Upper Peninsula, and into Wisconsin and Minnesota.

But then I handled three fatal motorcycle accidents in about six weeks, as a seasoned ten-year police officer in the fall of 1984. I never got back on that Honda and sold it the next year. For 28 years I did not ride a motorcycle. I was a police officer for 32 years, the latter half as a Detective-Sergeant. I retired in 2006 and became a licensed Professional Investigator. In 2011 when I was battling breast cancer, the trauma and fear that goes with it, I remembered the freedom and joy of riding my Honda way back when, and this was about the time that trikes began showing up on the highway.

My friend Jackie Smith gave me the pathway back to my love for riding motorcycles. She is a hairdresser and we started playing golf together a long time ago and have been friends ever since. In the spring of 2012, she bought a 2009 Harley-Davidson Ultra-Classic Trike, deciding that three wheels were better than two for her. She told me about it at golf and offered to take me for a ride. She picked me up one day, that awesome wind therapy hit me, and I was captivated again by the emotion that I felt riding my Honda 28 years ago. Jackie picked me up several times that summer and we rode all over Lower Michigan. Finally, towards the end of summer of 2012 it was time for me to get my own trike.

Jackie is an adored fan of Harley-Davidson and all of the bling that comes with it. I however, was not, so I went to Ray C's Extreme store in Lapeer, anything but Harley-Davidson. Ready for my care and attention, waiting on display, was this beauteous white 2012 CanAm Spyder RT Limited, floor model with 1970 miles on the odometer. I remember the miles because that was the year I graduated from high school. At this point, September of 2012, I was turning 60 years old and was one year cancer free. I bought this classy white bike and the matching white trailer as a birthday present. Happy Birthday to me!

In late October, Jackie and I took a 3-day weekend and rode to Tennessee to experience the adventure of the Tail of the Dragon. This is the number one road for motorcycles to ride on in the United States. It is 11 miles of roadway with 318 curves in the edge of the Smoky Mountains. It was crazy to ride that road, breathtaking the first time through at speed limit, and heart stopping on the way back, like a roller coaster. A marvelous experience on those stupendous curves. We drove 12 hours in the cool rain on Friday to get to Tennessee, spent Saturday riding around on The Tail and the mountains, all in damp, cool weather. The temperatures had dropped significantly in Michigan and by the time we returned on Sunday I nearly froze to death. We rode in the vicinity of 1400 miles that weekend. That's how the craziness started.

In the Beginning

That white CanAm Spyder RT Limited became a beloved friend. For eight years we traveled around the United States, riding in 19 states and Ontario, Canada, fascinated with the variety of the land forms, the towns and the people.

By 2020 the fascination has turned into a passion to ride in all 49 states of the Continental United States and all 10 provinces of Canada. I decided to go big, choosing the furthest state in the United States, Alaska, as my next quest. Riding to Alaska would mean I would encompass four Canadian provinces and five more states of the United States. The allure of riding to Alaska would involve time and endurance, a captivating challenge.

I asked my trusted friend Jackie if she wanted to join me on this wild, month-long endeavor to ride to Alaska. She was over the moon with excitement and the planning began at that moment, June 1, 2020. A year of planning, a year of excitement, intrigue, detailed maps and routes, collecting our gear. There was one looming shadow in the planning. We were dead into the Covid-19 pandemic and the borders between Canada and the United States were closed. We were sure that all would be back to normal by the day we leave, July 1, 2021.

The trip to Alaska became our obsession, and we were going to plan it meticulously. We both pored over maps, paper and computer, determining routes from Michigan to Alaska. At first it seemed like a far-off dream that would become a realty as we planned and scrutinized the maps. Maps became friends, enticing us to explore their environment and their challenge. We were only going to have 31 days to complete the trip, so the planning has to be precise, organized, well laid out. In June 2020 we both spent hours pouring over maps, both map books and Google maps on the computer, planning routes according to milage. We planned the route according to towns with motels.

Since we were staying in motels it made sense that we travel as light and simple as possible, conserving gas and weight. Since we decided that my matching trailer would stay home, I needed a large dry-bag that would strap to my back seat and expand or diminish as needed. On June 24 at the REI Store in Troy, I was elated to find a large dry-bag, the perfect size, orange in color contrasting to my white bike, for visibility and safety. It would hold my computer tablet and charging cords, pouches of popcorn, extra jackets, shoes, water and my laundry bag. Since this was my first purchase for the trip, it felt special, like this trip is really going to happen.

As we planned this 10,000-mile trip, we figured that we would have to ride 400 to 500 miles a day to make it all the way out to Alaska and back, in 31 days, and have time for some sightseeing. On July 17, 2020 it was 88 degrees, we decided to take a 500-mile test run. We rode to the Mackinaw bridge via US23, along Lake Huron, across the bridge and back, then down I-75 to home. On the way back down I-75 at about 400 miles we stopped at a rest area south of West Branch and I walked around for five minutes. That was all I needed and the next 100 miles were easy. We determined at that point that we could handle traveling 500 miles in a day and still have time to rest and relax. Little did we know that 500 miles a day could be endless in difficult terrain and tedious weather.

We realize that communication is the life blood between Jackie and I as we travel safely mile after mile, bonded together with each other's voice always in our ear. On our past local trips, we communicated through our CB radios and put up with a multitude of problems, feedback from other CB's, wind on microphone, and Jackie's microphone key on her clutch hand. At this point there were several new wireless intercom systems for motorcycles, and we were thankful that we found the Cardo Pack Talk system, which was highly rated. This system was like a reassuring friend that allowed us to talk to each other at any time through our earphones. That reassurance was like a miracle to family that could reach us through our personal phones connected to the Pack Talk system. Each of us was able to answer our phone calls without sharing the conversation, and listen to our personal music on Pandora, through the phone, through the helmet, without the other hearing the music. If either of us spoke, the volume on the music instantly turned down, then came back up after speaking. We could be at least a half mile apart and still hear clearly. The only down side to all of this is that if one of us is on a personal phone call, we lose communication with the other rider. What a miracle of technology that kept us happy, centered and safe through our trip.

Up until now I did not have individual stationary holders on my handlebars for my telephone or water bottle. I knew that finding the right ones would be imperative for safe travel. I searched thoroughly on line, ordered them, and waited patiently for my newest purchases. I installed the water bottle holder myself, but my neighbor Dan loosened the center bolt on the bike for the phone holder attachment. In order to keep the phone charged while riding for hours and hours, I bought a six-foot charging cord to run from the USB port in the frunk (front trunk) to the phone holder. A little excited with my fix, I had to remember that during rain both the phone and charging cord had to be tucked away.

I was eager to test my new equipment, so I met Jackie on July 31, on a nice summer day for a 345-mile ride. The adjustable phone holder and charger were flawless. No jiggle, no vibration and I could clearly see the phone without blocking my view of the gauges. However, the water bottle holder was a different story. As I went over a bump in the road, my blue plastic bottle bounced out and went air born. I stopped and retrieved the pieces for the trash. Over the next few months, it was a bit of a game. Different variations of bottles, trying to find one that would hug the holder, went helter-skelter into the wind several times and filled the trash. I decided that I had to be patient and find a heavier, more expensive holder to make the trip.

When I proudly bought my bike back in 2012, I bought a top-flight heavy white leather riding jacket, bordered with some red and black. Now 2020, the colors are dull and the leather is worn. Getting a little tight (must be shrinking in the dryer), it was time for a new jacket for this trip. Wearing leather on a 2-wheeler is an assumption, but tipping over a 3-wheeler is practically non-existent. The new textile, mesh fabrics, lighter, more comfortable for long journeys, are now available. I liked the jacket as soon as I saw it on line, and it was only half price. Sold by CanAm, it is white with raspberry insets with fancy swirly stitching in white, and black piping. Again, I waited patiently for its arrival, all these presents for the trip arriving in the mail. It was like it was made for me; I can imagine it becoming my trademark for the trip. I absolutely love this riding jacket.

Suddenly in August 2020 I realized that my 2012 CanAm Spyder RT Limited was starting to burn a little oil. We had happily traveled together for 54,000 miles, like dear friends for eight years, since it marked the beginning of a new chapter in my life, turning 60 years old and cancer free. In the back of my mind was this little, niggling worry. No matter how beloved, I started questioning if she would be strong enough to handle this trip and the mountains. My doubts began to creep into this crazy idea to ride clear to Alaska. I had not thought about the 10,000 miles or the need for a larger gas tank, not to mention that it was air cooled instead of water cooled. She had done so well, earned a special place in my garage. It would be hard to let her go.

Checking out newer bikes almost felt like disrespect until the priorities of this trip took over. I did not want her breaking down in the middle of the trip. I learned about the upgrading of the RT Limited, found the motor is now 1300 cc, up from the 998 cc. The gas tank had been enlarged, bringing the range to 240 miles instead of my present 140 miles maximum. The 2020 model change of the RT Limited had awkward lines and angles, making it aesthetically unappealing. This was such a big step, so I just brooded on it for a couple of weeks, secretly starting to say goodbye to my trusted friend.

In September I decided that I really had to let her go in order to safely make this trip successful. My partner, Frankie, then presented me with a present for my birthday, $10,000 cash to put toward a newer motorcycle. She was keeping our cash stash; I had no idea just how much was there. After a few days to get over that surprise, the search was in full swing. In memory of my present RT Limited, I knew that my newer bike also had to be white. There were several used bikes for sale, individually and from dealerships. I was texting and emailing and doing some serious looking for a newer, low milage bike in Michigan or nearby states.

In late September of 2020, I was in Gaylord, Michigan golfing for a few days. On a whim on the way home, I stopped into the Extreme Sports store just to see what they had in stock. I parked right in front of the store and lo and behold, there was a newer white RT Limited looking at me. It was sitting there a little lost and out of place, forlorn and dusty, outside in the entry way. I could feel the appeal and my excitement knew no bounds. Hard to believe, it turned out to be a 2019 model with only 63 miles on it. No wonder it looked forlorn, she had been in the showroom for a year, waiting for me to arrive! Needless to say, the next day, on a cool autumn day perfect for departure and arrival, we rode the last 160 miles on my trusted friend up to Gaylord for the trade-in. We left her there, that's how goodbyes go. They gave me a good price and I knew the ride to Alaska was coming closer. I felt like I hit the jackpot: I gained 300cc, 100 miles more on a tank of gas, liquid cooling and a 6th gear.

With my new bike properly ensconced in her place in the garage, our trip was taking on epic proportions, even though it was nine months away. Our eagerness for this trip knew no bounds. Our exhilaration slowly grew with each new purchase. Jackie text me on October 6 and said there were 266 days to GO to July 1, 2021. We made a game of the days to departure. For the next nine months we kept a count-down of days, like a refrain, texting back and forth. Sometimes that was all the text said, other times it was the opening for whatever was important that day. It was a sliver of enjoyment, counting the days kept us centered in the dream of the trip.

October 11, 2020, we went for an all-day ride and had the ceremony of the bells. There is a story that if you have a small metal bell on your bike framing, the tinkling bell will keep you safe and the demons away. The bike owner must receive the bell as a gift. My original bell on my first bike, received as a gift from a good friend and fellow rider, had been transferred to this one on the day I bought it. This was the first time that Jackie admired my new bike and she presented me with a new bell from Open Road Girl, that I attached to the lower frame. Just before we left on the trip to Alaska my next-door neighbor presented me with another bell, a "Thin Blue Line" on a black flag, referring to my years as a police officer. The chorus of the bells will keep me safe.

I was intrigued with my purchase of a new trunk organizer. It was a bit of a puzzle, a black canvas belt of pockets, that connects under existing screws around the back and sides of the inside of the opening, above the flip shelf. There are velcro strips between the screws that you just apply to the wall of the trunk. I installed it on October 17, amazed that it fit perfectly and exactly as directed. It has several various sized pockets, some with covers and some without, some solid and some mesh. It was comforting and fun to organize all of the small stuff that is so important for this trip: pens, flashlight, scotch tape for routes, packages of Kleenex and wipes, pepper spray and refill, knife/tool, glasses holder, comb, and so on. I have a tendency to be a little OCD, so this organizer was exactly what I needed.

The backrest installation was not as comforting, but it certainly was interesting. In my journal I wrote, "lil sweat, lil swearing and a lot of adjustment". On November 6 I unpacked the box, was a little overwhelmed by the parts in the process. The garage was strewn all over with parts and I was trying to read the instructions. Independent as always, I did not call my neighbor Dan, who would have put the backrest together in no time flat. After much sweat and tears, I determined that the instructions were inaccurate. That was a major accomplishment and now I can figure it out myself. I learned way more about the seat of a Spyder Limited RT than I thought possible. I had an affinity for the backrest by the time it was completed and no parts were left over. I knew it would serve me well on the coming trip, 10,000 miles with a back rest, certainly is comforting, like a friend holding your back.

My CanAm Spyder RT Limited is brand new, only 63 miles, and winter is coming. Living in Michigan does not allow me to ride year-round. There is the worry that with only eight months until go, I need to get it broken in and the first 3,000-mile warranty oil change done before the trip. I tried to get as many miles on as possible before snow flew. I was lucky that on November 7th and 8th, it was unusually warm in Michigan so I rode both days, totaling 414 miles for the weekend. It was strange riding the bike just to see the miles go up. On November 9th the weather turned cold, I put the winter storage insurance on, ending the year with 1299.5 miles, trusting that next April through June will give me time for riding, to get the next 1700 miles on.

As winter came on, the Covid Pandemic was spreading wildly and getting a little worrisome. No vaccine yet and the United States and Canadian border was still closed. We were following every precaution, wearing masks and using hand sanitizers on every door we opened, and washing in between. On Thanksgiving Day, November 26, Jackie has come down with Covid-19. I am scared for her, worried that with the Covid and after-effects she will not be able to make the trip. She lost both her sense of taste and smell, and was bone weary tired. She slept for two weeks and I only heard from her occasionally in the evening, between sleeps. We wanted to help her and took a couple things, including Essentia Water to help with dehydration, leaving them on the front porch and calling to let her know it was there. After two weeks of sleep, there was Jackie back to work, as usual, suddenly recuperated, testing negative and now well rested.

On Sunday, December 13 we started working on our travel route. Sunday became a winter ritual, like going to church, mapping our route. With the snow falling and the winds howling outside the windows, it was reassuring that the trip was in progress, and we were happily immersed in it. The panorama of our overall trip to Alaska has already been established. Now is the time for me to do the close and immediate work of figuring out which roads, highways, and freeways we will follow between destinations and map it precisely. On a Sunday afternoon I would get started on the road scenario, run into questions, call Jackie for consultation. She would open up her computer and her maps, and we would compare and discuss and decide. Using the Google mapping program on my laptop and with my touch screen, it is amazing that I can bring the roads and towns in close and see the size, proximity to the highways, hotels, gas stations and restaurants. I also put a Find Distance program on my laptop that gives me the distance between any two points; by air, water and land. What an interesting way to spend a Sunday afternoon in winter during Covid surrounded by maps and possibilities. I am writing everything out by hand, then typing it all in the computer. Roads, turns, miles, towns, all of it. The intent is to have a day-by-day travel route all typed out and ready to go. Family will have a copy as well, for comfort and information. I am doing a few days at a Sunday session, sometimes several. It was intricate and exciting. 200 days to GO.

Life has a way of getting in front of my preoccupation with travel details.

My partner Frankie had a stroke on December 14, 2020. So, I was suddenly stopped up short, travel plans did not seem so all encompassing, after all. Initially the stroke left her unable to speak or swallow. Hospitalized for several days, her ability to swallow returned by the next day. As a retired English teacher, words were her friends for her whole career. So ironically when they left, she diligently worked to gather them home. The memory of words returned after about six weeks of daily practice, along with speech therapy. A series of tests during hospitalization uncovered previously unknown serious heart issues. Multiple medications became the norm and we had to dodge and genuflect the pharmaceutical companies about astronomical costs. We decided to transfer from a local cardiologist to the Beaumont Ministrelli Women's Heart Center in Royal Oak since we trusted their procedures. Another round of thorough and multiple tests that all came back positive. When this all started, I was highly concerned about her health and the trip was in jeopardy. We had a relaxing Christmas and by mid-January we decided to continue with the detailed plans for the trip. (There was a little niggling doubt in the back of my mind that maybe the trip would not truly happen, but finally by April, Beaumont gave her a good prognosis and we breathed a sigh of relief.)

Sunday winter rituals continue even as the weather got increasingly cold and nasty outside. On January 17, we were both cozy and warm inside, me preoccupied with the routing and Jackie engrossed in hotels. We were on the phone together multiple times. This precise planning gives us character and contentment, building excitement and anticipation for the trip. We want to know where we are going every day and have a destination at the end of the day. Jackie seems to enjoy looking at hotels and finding the best deals whereas I will continue to do all of the routing, mapping and mileage. She checked at Denali, Alaska and West Yellowstone, Montana and found that they are already filling up for July of 2021. So, she started making our first reservations today. Everything is subject to change because of the Covid-19, but we really don't believe it will change our plans.

On a blustery January 24, I spent another ritual Sunday afternoon finishing the routes, the biggest part of the job is done. Jackie is getting hotels lined up; then I add their addresses and directions to and from each hotel for each day. My intent is to write out the directions for the day on a 4"x 6" index card. There is a plastic pull-out card that slides in and out of the dashboard on my bike. I have found that an index card can be taped to the pull-out, and it will stay dry and protected while riding. I can easily pull it out and check directions. We just learned that Canada's borders will stay closed until February 22 because of Covid. We have been anxiously watching every month for the closures to be lifted; avoiding thinking about the possibility of having to go to Plan B for our trip. We cannot get to Alaska on wheels without going through Canada. Starting to become concerned, we are keeping the gremlins away by acting as though the trip will go on as planned. 158 days to GO.

Continuing to believe that the trip to Alaska will happen, I have booked our bus ride through the Denali National Park, to the tune of $325. We have been told by several people that this is one good way to see the park. Plus, it will give us a day off the bikes and just sight see without driving. On February 10, I received a recording from the Denali bus tour that they will only be having one tour a day instead of two, so our departure will be between 7 and 9am rather than 1pm. This is already booked and paid for. February 14 Jackie booked us on the Boat Cruise out of Seward, Alaska for July 13. It will be a whale watching cruise out into Resurrection Bay with lunch on Fox Island. I got us set up for the roundtrip train ride from Anchorage to Seward that day as well, about 1½ hours travel each way. Again, a chance to be off the bikes and enjoying the scenery more.

The bling and the people is one of Jackie's entitlements for taking in the Motorcycle Rally in Sturgis, South Dakota, which normally starts the first week of August. The Rally in 2021 is expected to bring in 500,000 motorcycles and the people that go with them. We realize that it would be a Covid spreader, to say the very least, and neither one of us wants to deal with that many people. So, our route planning has put us in Sturgis on July 24, 25 and 26, well before the mass of people arrive, but early enough for Jackie to savor the array of shirts, jackets, hats, leather, chrome and anything else Harley being sold there. Jackie called a few hotels in the Sturgis area, only to learn, crazily, that we better be reserving rooms right now because they fill up fast a year ahead.

With Sturgis on our list, we are reminded that we need to have protection along. Since I am a retired police officer and am licensed to carry a firearm for safety reasons, it is important to carry on the trip. However, upon further research I determined that carrying a firearm in Canada is not possible. Not a firearm, not a taser and not a stun gun. So now I have ordered us each a law enforcement grade pepper spray with refills. These can be kept close at hand and reassure us, should we find the need, helping us feel safe.

In early March the United States-Canadian border is still closed. In spite of that crowbar still looming before us, I continued to gather equipment. The orange dry bag that was my first proud purchase back in June gave me hope once again, that the trip will go on. In keeping with my plan to be as colorful and bright as possible, I ordered a red cargo webbing, 15" x 15", to hold the dry bag in place on my back seat. It came with several attached hooks that I thought would connect to my hand-holds on either side, but the hooks were too small. I searched high and low and finally, I found two large carabineers to connect to the multiple hooks on the cargo webbing. Then I will hook the carabineers to an adjustable wide strap around the back and just below the trunk lid. I will carry all of my clothes in a red rectangle canvas bag in the frunk (front trunk). This is more pliable and will hold a lot more than the formed leather luggage that came with the bike, complete with wheels and handle. Everything can be adjusted as the dry bag increases and decreases in size, depending on what's in it and how full the dirty clothes bag is getting.

Now that the mapping of our route is progressing happily, except for the border crossing question mark, and my bike is also happily well equipped and getting ready for the trip; we have to look at our own physical ability. We both have been working out diligently all winter, Jackie at the recreation center and me in my work-out room. Since last fall, by the end of golf season and driving the motorcycle, I was having significant pain in my left thumb. On February 23 a specialist injected the base of my thumb and I was also fitted with a brace to wear while driving. Since that left thumb is what I shift with, I started using the brace in the spring, found that it fits fine and takes the knuckle out of use. It also fits nicely in the cubby-hole in front of my motorcycle seat, when not in use.

Around the same time Jackie was limping and learned that both of her knees needed repair. The doctor picked the worst one and she had Arthroscopy surgery on her right knee on March 4. She went back to work on March 9, and except for some daily swelling for a couple of weeks, it improved significantly with a little ice and rest. She should have plenty of time to get it fully healed before the trip, and before golf starts up for that matter.

By March both Jackie and I are doing everything we can to be ready to travel in a few months. March 10 both of us got our first of two Covid vaccine shots. By the end of March, the Canadian-United States border closure has been extended until April 22. For the last 10 months, while we have been planning the trip to Alaska, the border has been closed. We continue to hope and diligently plan, in spite of the dream of riding to Alaska becoming more and more questionable with each passing month of extended border closures. The only other way to get our motorcycles to Alaska would be to take multiple ferries from Washington state, through the many islands off the west coast of Canada. That route would be time and cost prohibitive for us.

Spring arrived and it was time to awake my bike from her winter sleep. She has been covered up for 5 months during most of the trip planning. March 21 was a sunny, spring day, 67 degrees. Apprehensive about trying to start her, to my surprise and excitement, she started on the first try. It felt exhilarating to be out and riding, a prelude to the trip, even for a quick 26-mile loop, especially so in March in Michigan. I still have another 1675 miles to ride to get to the 3,000-mile warranty oil change before the trip. The next day was another fine spring day and I added 191 miles more towards my goal. However, it was early spring in Michigan, so it was mid-April before I could get more riding time in. Over the next two months, the Thumb of Michigan became a map that I followed, like a grid, to get to the 3,000-mile mark. I witnessed the tractors with plows and seed planters prepare the fields. Short rides in the fresh spring air, a hundred or so miles at a time, back and forth through the country side. Jackie did not want to join me for all those miles since her bike was ready and serviced for the trip.

Being back riding the bike I realize that my helmet is too tight, uncomfortable to wear for a 10,000-mile trip. After ordering a top-of-the-line, expensive helmet, I found that it not only did not fit, but it was made in China. I decided I liked the looks of the Nolan helmet, and was lucky enough to find the brand in a dealership in Rochester, Michigan, and fitted the proper size. They ordered my new white helmet. I feel like I can wear it for 500 miles each day, quite comfortably, especially with the Pack Talk intercom installed. The extra shade protection from the bill, as well as the dark eye shade that slides up inside, are important safety features for me.

April, 2021 turned out to be the cruelest month. The Canadian-United States border is still not open and no date in sight yet. Planning to ride to Alaska has been beyond exciting, the precise detail of the route has been worth every minute. The written route has become part of us, like a Bible. The thought of not being able to make this ride to Alaska is just unacceptable. I am still thinking that maybe, just maybe it is possible. In the meantime, we are talking about Plan B: which is to go southwest out to Las Vegas, north along the California-Oregon coast, and end up back in Washington July 19, as we had planned coming in from Canada, and pick up our initial route and reservations across the northern states. On April 7, I got my second Covid shot.

Change Of Plans

May 20, 2021, Canada announced that their border will remain closed until June 22. We cannot wait any longer, so have made the soul-numbing decision not to ride to Canada and Alaska, but to go southwest into the heat. All of those detailed plans, routing and reservations, of planning our dream trip to Alaska is gone. I am almost numb with disappointment. I want to believe that the trip to Alaska will wait for another time, so I will keep the planned routing that we established.

Now that we are not going to Alaska, we have to cancel several reservations. We each made contact with the reservations that we had set up and cancelled everything, the bus ride, the train ride, the boat ride and the hotels. Several things were paid for, but ultimately, we got back all but 10% on one reservation, losing about $32. We both feel fortunate that we are able to get most of our money back because several reservations had said "NO REFUNDS". We believe that we got our reservations refunded because the United States-Canada border was closed because of Covid.

In the meantime, looking on the brighter side, there are advantages to going southwest. Jackie's good friend Joanne, lives in Marana, Arizona and another friend Angie, is in Las Vegas, Nevada, so we will visit both of them. Furthermore, we can visit my nephew Joel and wife Sarah in Evergreen, Colorado, plus my niece Rachel, her husband and new son in San Diego, California. In spite of our grave disappointment, we are comforted by seeing friends and family in our plans.

I have rerouted the first 19 days to take us south and west through Indiana, Illinois, Missouri, Kansas and Colorado, and visit Joel and Sarah. From there we will head south into Albuquerque, New Mexico, then west into Arizona and the Grand Canyon. Planning to go down to Marana over night to visit Joanne, we will then go northwest up to Las Vegas, Nevada to see Angie. We intend to take a two-day loop out into Utah and back to Las Vegas, and then another two-day loop down to San Diego, California and back to Las Vegas. From there we will ride north up to Reno, Nevada and then northwest across northern California to Arcata. Then we will travel north along the coast into Oregon and be in Burlington, Washington on July 19. This zigzag route will hit many states that I have not ridden in, working on my endeavor to ride in all 49 states in North America. The routing was just as tedious, but finding the towns or cities to stay in much easier because of the population in the United States versus Canada. Jackie has worked a lot of hours to get us reservations in hotels along the way, and our overnight stays are established.

From Burlington, Washington we go back south and east to the Oregon border where we will go white water rafting on July 20. Then southeast to Twin Falls, Idaho, back northeast to West Yellowstone, Montana, through Yellowstone National Park and into Wyoming. East into Spearfish, South Dakota for a few days, then northeast to Devils Lake, North Dakota. The final three days will be back across northern Minnesota and Wisconsin, the Upper Peninsula of Michigan, across the Mackinaw bridge and back home on July 31. I have printed out the day-to-day directions in a font that allows me to cut out the print in a size to exactly fit on my 4"x 6" index cards. I have attached each day to a card, they are packed along with my computer tablet and other technical stuff.

In spite of our dismay and terrible disappointment, we are taking on the new route with trepidation because of the high heat and pending forest fires.

The last days are going quickly now as I make final preparations for my bike.

First, my new GPS needed to be installed. Neither the local dealership or the Gaylord dealership could do it in any kind of a timely manner, despite their initial promises. I was relieved that Dan, my reliable and talented neighbor, says that he will install the GPS. Among other things he is a small engine mechanic, and handy to check directions on U-Tube. On May 8 he found that a part was missing for the GPS mount, and one of the four center bolts was stripped; he had to tap it to get it out. The stripping had happened when I picked up this bike in Gaylord, when they moved the phone and cup holder from the old bike. Dan ordered the missing part and we were lucky it arrived two weeks. He finished the installation on May 23. 39 days to GO!

With only a little more than a month to lift-off, I am going over final notes in my mind to be sure that everything is ready to go. To test the GPS, I rode 253 miles on May 23, towards the goal of the 3000-mile break-in period. I was back into the helter-skelter of 10 months ago when water bottles seemed to become airborne quite quickly. This time the water bottle bounced out once again, ready for the trash, but I knew that a better quality, form fitting holder was on the way, back-ordered twice, so for now I have to be patient.

Because of the extreme heat which we will be expecting, the clothes that I wear on this trip to the southwest have to be coordinated for the heat. Also, on that day it was 83 degrees, low temperatures for the trip ahead. I was very comfortable in UV protection capris and short-sleeve shirt, a test to the weather and the minimal heat from the bike. I start planning my clothes for the trip minus several pair of jeans. Wearing capris, but not shorts because of skin burning and bugs, will be the norm. I will also pick up more shirts with UV protection for the higher temperatures. We have ordered cooling vests that will help in the extreme heat.

At the last minute, things are breaking down and we have to continue to be patient. Jackie and I went for a ride on June 6, a nice summer day, and almost immediately our Pack-Talk communication system would not sync together, no matter what we tried. If this happens on the trip we are doomed. Ultimately, we went to Dale's house, Jackie's son, and discovered that the receptacle on her modular was stuck on the end of the charger, so her set could not be charged, and it was dead. It meant that at this late date we had to replace part of her system. It was under warranty and they agreed to send the replacement out just as soon as they received the faulty one in the mail. We overnighted everything as they requested and two weeks later, June 20, we were elated and relieved to be able to communicate freely with the new modular on Jackie's helmet.

With all of those container ships stuck in harbors it's hard to imagine the patience you need to wait for little things like a mirror clip, the bottle holder, oil change kits as well as cooling vests. When installing the GPS, Dan snapped a clip holding the mirror, in order to get the side panel off. The clip is back-ordered so we have to wait. The kit that Dan needs to do the 3000-mile warranty oil change before I leave, has been back-ordered as well. In the meantime, I checked at another dealership, and was pleasantly surprised that they had several oil-change kits in stock. The dealership tells me that if I save the receipt and document the milage, that will qualify for warranty purposes.

The bottle holder has become a trash problem. A winter of research to every available water bottle holder on line, I found what I needed through La Monster. It was however, out of stock and back-ordered. I waited two months before it finally arrived. It was a Hallelujah day! Dan installed the bottle holder on

June 27. One stainless steel thermos bottle came with the holder and I bought two more, all with straws. I plan to stay hydrated in the extreme heat, will fill them all in the morning and carry the two extras in the trunk. That holder and those bottles became one of the most precious pieces of survival on this trip.

Things are moving to final preparations, and we are nervous but excited about leaving. And then in final conclusion I got a little light-headed and fainted in the bathroom on June 25, five days before leaving. I woke up and realized that I had hit my face on the shower base. A ride to the Emergency Room thankfully proved no fracture of the face, nothing serious and I will do some follow-up testing when I get back. An hour in ER and I am ready to go, good as new. However, I will be sporting a black eye for the most of the trip. Over the weekend I realized that my head and neck was out of alignment, and a chiropractor realigned it on Monday. On an 8,000-mile trip I would have been in dire pain without getting my head and neck straightened around. When I was in the Emergency Room, they did a CT scan of my head that revealed a previous neck fracture that is healed. The Chiropractor also did an x-ray that revealed the neck fracture. I am filled with bewilderment as to which violent incident caused that?

It has now been established: Canadian borders are not opening up until at least July 22. We have made the right decision. I guess there was a small part of me still expecting, dreaming to get to Alaska, in spite of the fact that we have established a new route. Disappointing doesn't even begin to describe how I felt. It is a let-down that I cannot explain. It was like mourning for the trip that could not be. A real mixture of feelings. I privately shed a lot of tears. I know that the trip to the southwest will be challenging but fulfilling in ways that we have not yet discovered. Going to Alaska and Canada was what I Really wanted to do.

June 27 and the final envelope of our leaving is now being packed. I will never be able to express the thanks I give to Dan for how he orchestrated so much to make this trip possible. On June 27 he did the 3,000-mile oil change. Now the bike is ready to go. It took me until June 20 to hit that milage mark. The cup holder had finally arrived in the mail; his final work was to attach it to my handlebars. Because the extreme heat has already settled in the southwest states, the cooling vests are in high demand, and have been back ordered once again. This time we will hope that they can arrive next week at Angie's house in Las Vegas when we are there for a few days.

On June 30 I do the final obligations for the trip. I mowed the lawn, two hours listening to music and ticking off the final list in my head. It was like an oblation to pack my belongings, I thoroughly enjoyed it. My red bag was filled with all of my daily clothes, and put in my frunk. I have a lot of hygiene products; it is important to take them all along for comfort! The right-side luggage suitcase is filled with hygiene products, whereas the left-side has my extra gloves, jackets, rain gear and such. My prized orange dry-bag is secured to the back seat holding all of the extras. As I finish packing, I am filled with exhilaration. Ready now for the trip of a lifetime, for 8,000 miles immersed in the sun, the wind, and the rain.

The Trip Southwest, USA

JULY 1, 2021
Lapeer, Michigan to Peoria, Illinois
481 miles

I was elated to begin my journey. Saying goodbye to my familiar surroundings, I had just a slight wonder if I would be back here again. Leaving on such an 8,000-mile journey is magical, and who knows where the magic will take us. I met Jackie at her house in Lapeer. We welcomed the trip by taking pictures of each other, with our bikes loaded to the maximum with everything that we will need for the coming 31 days. It was a cool, comfortable 65 degrees when we left Lapeer at 8:50am wearing our riding jackets, traveling the familiar freeway, west on I-69, out and away.

The miles already rolling beneath us, though not as comfortable as we would have liked. Michigan roads are known for needing repair, I-69 was in terrible shape south of Lansing. We were eager to be out of Michigan, leaving home behind us with the potholes and patches. Once we got to Indiana the roads were re-born, beautiful to behold, and now we know that we are really on the way out of Michigan. We turned off from I-69 onto divided Hwy 24 just south of Fort Wayne, our home for the next 260 miles, taking it all the way to Peoria, Illinois. This path will take us on divided highways, two-lanes with gravel shoulders, grassy shoulders, and no shoulders at all.

We were like a couple of kids, rejoicing in our new adventure, riding through numerous small towns and fields in bloom for as far as you could see. The corn was already head high and I could smell its sweet scent. I remember as a kid when "knee high by the 4th of July" was a good crop. After riding in the sun for about four hours, we were hungry and enthusiastic for lunch. I happened to spot this leafy little park along the Wabash River just west of Huntington, Indiana. Pleased, we found this peaceful place for our first lunch, with a couple of picnic tables, a two-person swing along the river's edge with a rosebush beside it, and a fire pit with big stones for seating. Taking a lunch break along the way will become the norm and we look forward to finding a restful place like this every day. The cooler on Jackie's back seat has the essentials for enjoyment. Along with bottles of water, Essentia water, and her Diet Pepsi for each day, on ice; there is bread, ham, cheese, mustard and mayonnaise, peanut butter and jelly, as well as paper products, to make substantial sandwiches. The seat of Jackie's bike is our preparation table to make them, then we eat at the picnic table overlooking the river. Comfortable in the shade, we were accompanied by the rippling water and happiness of the rose bushes.

Our ride continued, and home has already become a distant memory, as we soak in the surroundings of the country, the fields and the small towns. About 160 miles later in Fairbury, Illinois, a little town in farm country, we were glad to spot a welcome place, an ice cream store. Seeking out ice cream shops every day will also become a gratifying ritual. Jackie craves ice cream every day, and it has to be real ice cream, not flavored ice. She gets two scoops. Because of lactose intolerance, I get one scoop of yogurt or sherbet. By this time the temperatures were in the mid 80's so that cold feeling of the ice cream going down was most satisfying. Jackie had mint chocolate with a pretzel and I had a velvety chocolate yogurt. An old fellow in the ice cream shop intrigued me, wearing blue jeans, boots, flannel shirt and suspenders, in spite of the temperatures.

We continued on through the rolling hills of the countryside for another hour, loving the freedom of the farms and vast fields spread out before us. Traveling along the roadway we were in full sunshine next to the open fields, and in welcome shade in the towns from their tree-lined streets. After a full day of riding for eight hours, covering well over 400 miles, we stopped for a light dinner at the Cornerstone Family Restaurant in Eureka, Illinois. We were satisfied with the day and all of our detailed planning coming to fruition.

Only 20 miles further we arrived at our hotel, America's Best Value Inn, about 7pm, thankful to find rest in a clean and adequate hotel. After riding on the bike all day, I went for a walk, just making circles around the perimeter of a nearby Kohl's parking lot, remembering the sights, the sounds and the smells of this beginning day. When we left home this morning it was just 65 degrees and I started with my riding jacket on. The temperatures remained in the comfortable low to mid 80's all day long. We will later remember this as one of the most delightful days, once we got into the unbearable heat of climate change in the weeks to come.

7-1-21 Ready to Travel.

7-1-21. Park along Wabash River, Huntington, IN

JULY 2, 2021
Peoria, Illinois to Junction City, Kansas
485 miles

After a refreshing sleep we were eager to begin the next long day. The trip surrounds us now and home seems a long way off. The hotel in East Peoria did not provide any breakfast, so we were in search of food as we crossed the Illinois River, headed southwest on Hwy 24. A quick stop at a McDonald's sufficed for now, but it was not in a good area of town. We ate at the tables outside, relishing the warm morning air. We kept one eye on our bikes, wary of the people coming and going. We were anxious to get out of the city and on the open road.

Once we cleared the city of Peoria, we rode about 125 miles on Hwy 24 to Quincy, Illinois, with green pastures, cattle and crops, like a painted landscape. We joined the rhythm of the rolling hills, continuing mile after mile, all 2-lane with partial shoulder to grassy shoulder to no shoulder at all. The best picture that I missed taking was when we were riding enclosed between two head-high corn fields, on a narrow two-lane road with no buildings or power lines in sight anywhere. Having to cover nearly 500 miles today, we felt the urgency to keep riding, soaking up the warm summery scenery as it unfolded before us.

We were in luck for lunch as we came across a shady roadside park, outside Mt. Sterling, Illinois across from a pretty horse farm. We savored our sandwiches, thankful to be free in this environment, in the coolness of the surrounding shade. The umbrella of the mature maple trees was a great canopy for us and for the red buildings surrounded by freshly painted white fencing; a mild scent of horses in the distance.

We crossed the expanse of a quarter mile bridge over the Mississippi River at Quincy to enter Missouri. This bridge was undergoing some construction so the traffic was backed up, we had time to absorb the brown flow of the river. We continued southwest on Hwy 24 all the way to Lexington, Missouri, rolling across the approximate 188 miles of 2-lane highway. We were surprised and pleased that we were again enveloped in the countryside of undulating hills, fields and small towns like we had ridden through all morning in Illinois. My head is on a swivel. I absolutely love meandering through the towns and farms, just looking at everything, like a picture. From falling down old farms long abandoned, to the large homes in towns, to the mansions on acreage in the country.

Being out in the flowing wind of motorcycle riding I especially appreciated the freedom and variety of smells today. Lots and lots of people were mowing grass as this was Friday before the 4th of July holiday. I took in the most prevalent scent of fresh cut grass, but then add to it manure, the occasional dead animal, smoke from a fire, fresh-cut hay, cigarettes, and every-once-in-a-while a whiff of pot. In one small town an old man was watering his vast array of potted flowers on and around his front porch, there were so many that I could smell those too. We called out to him how nice they looked, he smiled and waved.

Looking for a break and a supper meal, we rode into Carrollton, Missouri, a town of about 3700 population, around 4:30pm. As we stopped at a traffic light downtown, we called out to a lady crossing the street, she told us a good place to eat was the River Bottom Brewing Co. We proudly parked our bikes on the main street right out in front and went inside. Once we ordered we were politely asked to move our bikes out of sight, around the block, off the main street. They were blocking it off at 5pm for a car show, that was in full swing by the time we left. They said the local brew was beautiful, frothy and foamy. We passed it by and concentrated on our hot sandwiches. In our world, driving a motorcycle and drinking alcohol does not mix.

At dinner we had already come 325 miles, realizing that we had another 160 miles to get to our hotel at Junction City, Kansas. According to my computer our average speed was 49 miles an hour, so we needed to deviate from our planned route, get to I-70 sooner to finish the ride. The terrain continued to be tumbling hills with pastures and crop farming until Kansas City. After that there was lots of grazing cattle and huge ranches off in the distance. The size of the hills increased about 15 miles east of Junction City, and they are becoming more frequent.

The most surprising thing that we enjoyed today, and were a part of, happened in Kansas City. About 6:30pm on the freeway traffic was backed up, stop and go, for about three miles. We finally came to an exit where 90% of the traffic was getting off. I saw above me over the freeway, a falling parachute, and just on our left was the Kansas City Royals baseball stadium. With elation I watched the parachute, with NAVY in blue on yellow, headed to land in the stadium. Later I realized that Jackie, who was driving behind me, saw three parachutes falling.

We arrived at our Best Western Hotel about 9pm, tired but thrilled that we have covered 345 miles on surface roads. Feeling exhilarated from a day of undulating hills and green pastures, with the temperatures warm and comfortable, in the mid 70's to low 80's. Somewhere along the way I recognized just how comfortable I was riding with capris and a light t-shirt, both with UV protection, my daily wear with the temperatures anything in the 70's or above. When we were unloading, I was completely amazed by the amount of luggage we have between the two of us. To see the bikes fully loaded, we don't realize how much gear we have until we see it all unloaded and stacked high on the hotel cart.

7-2-21 Crossing the Mississippi at Quincy, IL

7-2-21 Loaded bikes

7-2-21 Lunch at the park

JULY 3, 2021
Junction City, Kansas to Denver, Colorado
488 miles

We started the day excited, looking forward to visiting my nephew Joel, high in the mountains in Evergreen, Colorado, later this evening. First, we have another long haul, another 470 miles to get to Denver. We had begun to realize by this third day of traveling, that 500 miles is excessive. During our planning we had discussed the number of miles, thinking that we should ride longer days in the beginning of the trip when we were fresh, well rested. We had forgotten about how important it is to stop and admire the scenery. However, it was a good day to ride that far, a straight shot across the freeway on I-70.

The morning started out across flat, open fields, a real patchwork of greens, browns and yellows, peaceful like a painting we were riding through. The sky was filled with cumulus clouds, fluffy and white, with windmills in the distance. The landscape was wide open terrain with a variety of field crops and pastures the whole way. Where there was the shade of a group of trees, there were buildings. We passed an old, abandoned farm close to the freeway. High weeds and peeling paint, it looked forlorn, except for a damaged blue fiberglass silo leaning to one side, dancing in the wind.

Riding across the plains of Kansas reminds me of my trip with my partner in 2017 when we rode west to east across this stretch of highway coming from South Dakota. Like Dorothy in the Wizard of Oz, there were nasty, treacherous winds out of the south, throwing us about. That day Frankie was literally holding her helmet on with one hand and gripping the handhold with the other. We were pulling the trailer and I didn't realize how hard I was leaning into the wind until we crossed a cement bridge overpass, the four-foot wall stopped the wind. The right front tire of the bike actually crossed the white fog line, a heart-stopping moment before I could wrench the bike back into the lane.

Today the wind is minimal, a pleasure to ride in, seeped in warmer temperatures, between 83 and 87 degrees and mostly sunny. Just outside of Denver it clouded up and rained all around us, but not on us. We rode on some wet pavement, never got rained on directly, though we would have welcomed the cool rain. This was a great day to listen to music, there wasn't much traffic and we were on straight freeway all day. I put the cruise on 75mph and the miles flew beneath us. We are using the Pack Talk Slim intercom in our helmets. Since we both have Pandora on our phones, we are listening and daydreaming. I listen to my 70's and 80's rock and roll, Jackie loves her country western.

Along the flat plains of Kansas, in one five-mile stretch, I saw the most recognizable symbol of American petroleum, the pumpjack. The pumpjack is known with colorful names like the nodding donkey, thirsty bird, rocking horse, and grasshopper. I was mesmerized, the humble pumpjack, one of the most durable and reliable machines ever conceived, were each about a half mile apart. All of the dozen pumpjacks I saw had an electrical box connected to it, except for one, where there was a residential sized propane tank and two solar panels, but no electrical box.

Our route to the hotel through the City of Denver was at the peak of rush hour and a bit tedious, after having spent the day at high speed on the open freeway. We arrived at the Quality Inn and Suites in Lakewood around 5pm, on the west side of Denver just off from Hwy 285. We unloaded our belongings, eagerly anticipating our first visit with family, Joel and Sarah at their home in Evergreen. We cleaned off the road grime, changed our shirts, powdered our faces and were back on the bikes in no time flat with enthusiasm.

Rode west on Hwy 285 and turned off at the edge of the Rocky Mountains, onto roads that were much like the "tail of the dragon" in Tennessee. The approximate 12 miles to their house was exhilarating, slow, winding and up-hill all the way. Their home on 2.5 acres on the side of a mountain above 7200 feet elevation, was extraordinary, comfortable and inviting. The mountain tops around them are part of their family. Sarah points her phone camera at the mountains identifying the name of each one. Their wooden, multi-leveled home with two decks, is surrounded by stands of pine trees with stunning vistas overlooking the mountains. Joel recently removed trees here and there in order for them to have more of a view of the distant mountains. They live emersed in nature, elk and deer feed in their yard and feel comfortable near the house.

They greeted us into their home, shared their joy and enthusiasm for living up here as they showed us through the house, the three levels of the back of the house in windows, welcoming the mountainside. The four of us drove into Evergreen, a town full of mountain adventures and scenic beauty. We stopped once to admire a large buck with an even larger rack, just off the road. We ate at the Black Hat Cattle Co., a rustic setting filled with western folk art, upscale, warm, cowboy atmosphere with a large shaggy bison head watching over the diners. Sarah, Jackie and I savored the clean beef flavor of our steaks while Joel relished a vegetarian meal. In the slowed-down, warm cowboy hospitality, we lost track of time as conversation flowed between us. We suddenly realized that we were the last customers and the restaurant was closed when we left.

It was dark by the time we said good-bye to Joel and Sarah, left to ride back to the hotel. Thank God for GPS, or a mountain lion would have eaten us. We only had to turn around once and thankfully avoided the cliff edges. Back at the hotel, half hour later, the evening was warm and comfortable, perfect for walking. Jackie and I walked around a multiple block square that we quickly realized was not level, mostly uphill, laboring. Evening sprinklers were on and the coolness of the water felt good as we walked in the spray. When we got around to the final leg of the block, we found that there was no sidewalk, but it was downhill. The choice was to walk on the edge of the 5-lane street or on a path of high weeds, so we did both. Probably a little more than a mile, definitely more than Jackie wanted to do, but it was satisfying.

We spent the whole day crossing the plains of Kansas and eastern Colorado, with no shade to be found. We ended the day high in the shade of the Rocky Mountains, in the fellowship and fun of family. We are tired but content with the fullness of the day.

7-3-21 A view from Joel's deck

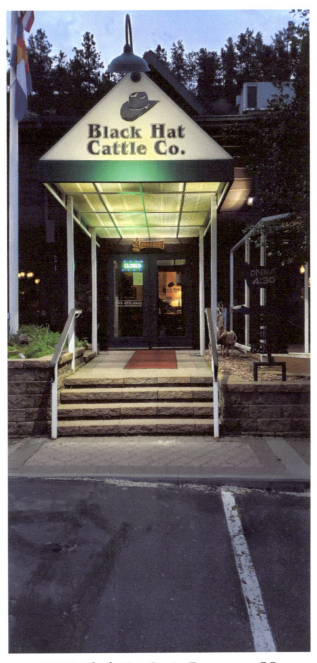

7-3-21 Black Hat Co. in Evergreen, CO

7-3-21 The plains of Kansas

JULY 4, 2021
Denver, Colorado to Albuquerque, New Mexico
433 miles

We celebrated America, Independence Day, the Fourth of July, by riding from Lakewood, Colorado to Albuquerque, New Mexico. We both wore American flag shirts for the day, beginning our celebration. We took Hwy 285 out of the Denver area southwest over the mountains, down across the valleys and scrub lands, mostly grazing farm land with the mountains in the distance on both sides. The gap between the mountains kept widening all the way into New Mexico. All of the homes were poverty level at best. Once in a while there would be a large ranch way off in the distance. I expected herds of cattle grazing, but there were only a few gathered around the water holes.

As we were coming down out of the mountains on Hwy 285, after it became just two-lanes, we had our first scary near-miss accident. I was leading with at least one car behind Jackie, as we were coming through a blind curve, around a rock face. As we cleared the rock-face we met a line of several vehicles with two trucks already passing the line, coming head-on at us. In an instant I accessed the situation: there was only about a half-width of shoulder, then a lot of rock. I slammed on the brakes and dove for the shoulder as both of the trucks forced their way back into the line of traffic, with everybody slamming hard on their brakes. Only an instant, that's how long it takes for a major accident. In this instant nobody got hurt and we all continued on our way. It surely left me shaken. A couple of fools in a hurry endangering the lives of so many.

We sped along, crossed into New Mexico without fanfare. I was struck by how the sign entering into the state was small and obscure, as well as all of the road signs throughout the state. The terrain went from green fields and pastures to brown brush and stone. All was fascinating to me, watching the changes happen as we traveled south. Just into New Mexico stood the San Antonio Mountain, a huge, dome-like mound that really is round on the top. I noticed that the mountains in Colorado support all of the trees, everything is lush green, whereas in New Mexico the mountains are brown stone and support only scrubby brown shrubs.

Before we left this morning I checked the mapping, realizing that Taos is only about 10 miles from our planned route. Kim Beyer, a friend from home, told us about the town of Taos and was adamant that we visit there. We were riding across desolate land with not much population when all of a sudden there were the strangest looking buildings on our left. Turned out it was Earthship Biotecture, a building company that uses existing natural and repurposed materials to build with, such as earth filled tires, bricks made from the local dirt, and glass blown from sand. We were captivated by this use of recycled material. There were at least a dozen buildings on maybe 50 acres, that were all made from the earth. We were unable to visit because they were closed but Earthship Biotecture is actually a school where you can stay for a month, learn to use the natural or repurposed products available.

Just another mile further we stumbled onto the Rio Grande Gorge Bridge. With little fanfare, all of a sudden there is this bridge over this very deep gorge, the Rio Grande River running through the bottom. We drove across it, parked on the other side, got off to walk out on the bridge and take pictures. The gorge is about 600 feet deep, that's a long way down. That might be the first time that I stood on something as solid as that bridge, but when I looked down I felt dizzy. I hung onto the railing. Heights never bothered me before.

As we drove along the way we saw lamas grazing at the side of the road, and old house trailers with old motorhomes or travel trailers attached to them. Kim was right, we were enthralled by the town of Taos itself, situated in the southwest corner of the Taos Indian Reservation. Made entirely of adobe, multi-storied homes are still occupied today, embodying living cultures of the Native American community. A welcome town, we were in search of some shade since temperatures remained in the mid 80's all day. We found most restaurants were closed because of the holiday, but we relished a good hamburger sitting at a red table under the shade of large trees, watching a couple of refurbished antique cars. Seeing the antique cars in this "old world" town seemed appropriate. The streets were lined with people as we drove out of town, with the Fourth of July parade beginning behind us.

We continued on towards Albuquerque via Hwy 68, back to Hwy 285. This road followed all along the Rio Grande River for nearly 50 miles. A refreshing ride in the early evening light. We stopped in Santa Fe, and when I tried to get a light shirt out of my front trunk, actually called a frunk, it would not open. To my consternations, we both tried again, again, again but that frunk had made up its mind, it was not opening. So now I'm sweating and swearing a little bit, thinking about finding a CanAm dealer to get the frunk open. We finally left it alone and drove on. 64 miles later, by the time we got into

Albuquerque, Wa-Lah! It opened up on the first try. I will never know what that was all about, but it's a lesson learned in leaving things alone.

The charm and entrancement of nature's beauty managed to slow us down, so the last 50 miles of scenery disappeared, we rode after dark. But the magical spell-binding of the fireworks in the distance beckoned us now. At the same time a thunderstorm was developing over the mountains to the southeast of the city. While the sun was setting off to the west, lightening was striking opposite it, with the fireworks flying in between. We were so lucky to be out, enveloped in this panorama of color, celebrating the Fourth of July. I lost count of the dazzling fireworks that coil, spin, spiral, whirl, burst, shoot, spatter, gush, rain, whizz, or zoom in the sky over the city ahead of us. I had to convince Jackie that the fireworks were not because of our arrival. But then, as we came into Albuquerque on the raised freeway, one all-encompassing firework explosion glittered and shimmered right beside us. Jackie laughed and proved I was wrong.

We were high and elated when we arrived at the hotel. Mesmerized by this Fourth of July panorama we unloaded before any rain hit. It was a day of celebration, in spite of the fact that we had to travel mute, Jackie and my helmets would not sync together from the beginning, regardless of what we tried. Taking the detour to Taos, we were thankful for navigating the town, the Rio Grande gorge and Earthship Biotecture, even though we could not communicate. Throughout the celebrating panorama of fireworks and storm pending, Jackie and I could not express our euphoria and enjoyment. We rode all day without communication.

This turned out to be one of the greatest days of our trip, but we were unable to express to each other what we were seeing or what we wanted to do. I was determined that this was not going to happen again. I tackled the problem that evening, did some serious reading, discovered the very simple thing that we overlooked and corrected it. Using the Pac Talk system, both helmets have to either be on Bluetooth, blue light, or DMC Group, green light. If they are not on the same frequency they will not sync. It works best on the DMC Group rather than Bluetooth. For the rest of the trip, communication became our celebration.

7-4-21 Earthships wall

7-4-21 Earthships

7-4-21 Our luggage that we carry

7-4-21 Rio Grand Gorge

7-4-21 Shaded seating w antique cars.

JULY 5, 2021
Albuquerque, New Mexico to Williams, Arizona
379 miles

As we rode west on I-40 the temperatures were in the mid 90's, our first day with higher-than-normal temperatures. We were slowly rising in elevation, so the terrain changed too, from brown scrubby to lush green and more cattle grazing. Our views were across vast areas of desert and pastures. The whole day we traveled on the freeway, so our speeds were higher, making the heat more tolerable. We carried lots of water that I diluted with Essentia Water, keeping my electrolytes up in this heat.

In New Mexico, between Thoreau and Coolidge, we stopped for gas and rested a little in some shade. It provided a good place to take pictures across the vast open landscape, showing lots of shades of pinks and browns. An old covered wagon advertising the Continental Divide at this point, establishing that we were at 7295 feet of elevation. This is the highest ground on the continent that allows water runoff either to an ocean or lower lands. At a shop I bought a souvenir to remember the Divide, a small red stone with a copper caricature of an Indian, made by hand by the local Navajo Indians. The grainy sand stone has brown lines running through it and is a pictorial of the area. As it was delicate, they packed it well; when it got shipped home it arrived all in one piece. A couple weeks later when we were in West Yellowstone, Montana, I talked to a guy from Texas that was riding a dirt bike on the Continental Divide from the southern border to the northern border of the United States. Having just been at this point on the Divide, I understood what an unbelievable undertaking this would be.

We crossed into Arizona and rode through the Petrified Forest National Park. As seniors we only paid $20 for an annual pass into all National Parks in the United States. The entrance to the park was actually a freeway exit, as the freeway goes right through the park. It was a 28-mile ride through colors that varied with the depths, a combination of browns, pinks, blues and greens were just mesmerizing. Of course, our speed was low, so the temperatures hovering around 100 degrees, lack of shade was beginning to take its toll. We were just plain hot. Also, the park had little or no trees, absolutely no shade anywhere, except for a few covered cement picnic tables at turnouts. We stopped to eat for some cement shady relief from the sun. The park was beautiful, but also rough, almost unwelcoming because you know you could not live there, even though there are over 400 species of plants and 200 species of birds. At the exit area we stopped and took pictures of some petrified wood, looking like cut tree trunks. These are fossils formed from living trees 225 million years ago. We were amazed, incredible to see that the wood turns to stone. This was the last place for a little shade and a little breeze before leaving the park.

The park road took us in a southwesterly route, ending on the local 2-lane Highway 180 with another 25 miles back to the freeway, through the Hopi Indian Reservation. As we came into the town of Holbrook there was a two-lane traffic backup, so I pulled up next to a tanker for a moment's relief in its shade. It blocked the fire of the sun for a few minutes. We stopped for gas and ate ice cream, cool and refreshing, inside in the air conditioning. Parched and burning up, the chocolatey taste and feel of the cold ice cream going down inside my body, in this heat, was exhilarating.

With renewed energy, onward and upward we went, through Flagstaff in the mountains. For the last hour as we rode higher, the trees became lush and green, reminding me of Northern Michigan. Though the shade was out there beyond reach, we rode in the full sun. Arriving at our air-conditioned hotel in Williams, a tourist town along the old Route 66, was more than a relief, after the endless sun of the day. After sufficiently cooling down we went in search of dinner, decided on a Mexican restaurant. I had the best tacos ever, fresh cooked meat and refried beans, not from a can. We picked up a few groceries before riding back to the hotel.

I needed to check the oil on my bike and in order to do that it has to be at running temperature. After dinner I took off, went up onto the freeway and drove quickly back 3 miles to the first exit, made a loop and came back around for a second pass. On the first trip I blew the cobwebs out. On the second trip I was going the proper speed and out of nowhere, behind me was a state trooper with lights on. I started to pull over as he blew by me and got off at the exit ahead. Of course, I thought I was getting pulled over, but was very glad he had not caught me on the first pass. Then within seconds none of it mattered because I was not the target. The oil level was fine.

Today I ticked off two more states, New Mexico and Arizona, on my quest to ride in all states and provinces in North America. The temperatures ranged from the high 90's to 101 degrees today, making it burdensome to admire the panoramic views and scenery, when all we are longing for is some shade.

7-5-21 Continental Divide

7-5-21 Petrified Wood Stump

7-5-21 Red Terrain of the Petrified National Forest

JULY 6, 2021
Touring around the Grand Canyon
131 miles

We rode these miles on a very HOT day. We started out at about 93 degrees, but as the day progressed it got to 107. The shade from intermittent clouds were our savior. The Canyon was about 55 miles north of our hotel at Williams, Arizona. Our route was three miles east on the freeway, then two-lane Hwy 64 all the rest of the way. I noticed on the way up that the grass was brown and dry, whereas the trees and shrubs were plentiful, green and lush. But the further north we rode the trees thinned out to almost complete barren land. Then as we got near the Grand Canyon the trees began to appear again and by the time we got into the park it was full forest. It was quite obvious that the forest floor is being cleared of dead wood and debris, no doubt for fire control.

Just outside the park entrance at the town of Tusayan, we needed a break from the heat, so we took in the Canyon Imax show "The Hidden Secrets". Honestly, the building was air conditioned and that was the main reason to go inside. The show was a documentary about John Wesley Powell and his crew who first mapped the Grand Canyon in 1869. They traveled in four boats along the Colorado river and through the rapids. I found it very informative and a copy of the video made it back home.

As we rode into the park, I experienced the most spectacular views that I have ever seen. The size and depth of the Canyon, a mile deep, 270 miles between the north and south rims, and 18 miles across, leaves one awestruck. A mixture of greens, browns, and pink colors, changed dramatically with the sun shining on the canyon walls, to red, orange and golden shades. With the depths and distances, the beauty of the view left me speechless. I was able to stand out on a rock, very carefully, unprotected, overlooking the rim and the whole Canyon. The vast space alone is not measurable to the naked eye. If you add all of the rest of the view, it is unlike anything else seen in the United States.

We rode to two or three viewing locations, but the traffic was slow and it was just too hot to be on a motorcycle. We were there for a couple of hours enjoying the atmosphere and excitement of other tourists, but we reluctantly had to let it go. The heat was so brutal and oppressive that we headed back to our air-conditioned room in Williams, Arizona. The Grand Canyon is a place to explore and celebrate in October, but not in July.

As we rode back down Hwy 64, near an area with a few buildings, Jackie spotted a "tree". I was ecstatic, thinking it was going to be a place for shade. But to my surprise, it was a cell tower that was covered with plastic pine tree branches to disguise it's look. It really was a work of art, towering against the clouds in the background. I don't know if we would have noticed the tower if we were riding in a car, because of looking up to the top of the tree and noticing the antennae cells.

As the day passed with its burdensome heat, we had a little blood pressure rise for both of us. We had another "near miss" today. Some fool was trying to pass us as we were traveling about 62 in a 55mph zone, over a slight rise. Sure enough, there was oncoming traffic. I saw the car coming from behind to pass us, just about the same time that Jackie yelled. We both took the right shoulder as far as we could, which wasn't much, without hitting rocks and going completely off the road. The oncoming vehicle was also braking hard. The last I saw in my mirror was the two vehicles stopped facing each other head-on, straddling the roadway and the shoulder in the southbound lane. The rocks prevented either vehicle from going further off without crashing. A few miles further the same fool came flying by us again, this time with no oncoming traffic, and he disappeared. Maybe this extreme heat is getting to this driver?

After this episode of a "near miss", Jackie and I discussed our heightened awareness while riding a motorcycle. Riding at this level of consciousness, mindful caution of danger, carefully watching and guarding is part of the gratification I get from riding, from taking a trip like this. Enduring this heat, the road conditions, the vehicles in my vicinity and seeing the sights is a feeling of freedom. Wind Therapy. Now if we could just get some Shade Therapy . . .

The hotel was a welcome comfort after the tremendous heat of the day and we were thankful for it. As temperatures are getting dangerously high, and forest fires are increasing, what are we to do? We realize that the main cause of this global heatwave is from the emission of greenhouse gases, being mostly carbon dioxide and methane. Burning fossil fuels for energy use creates most of these emissions, but cement production, agriculture, steelmaking and forest loss add to it as well. The rise of temperatures is affected by climate feedback such as the loss of sunlight-reflecting snow cover, and the release of carbon dioxide from drought-stricken forests.

However, we were very disappointed that we could not spend more time at the Grand Canyon. It was just too hot to be outside at all, much less on a motorcycle. This was our second day of experiencing this excessively intense heat, and clearly the worst. Today it got to 107 degrees, that is sweltering to ride in. Even at riding speed it saps the liquid right out of you, no matter how much our electrolytes got replaced.

7-6-21 Cell Tower Tree

7-6-21 Grand Canyon view 2

7-6-21 Grand Canyon

7-6-21 Nancy on the Rim of Grand Canyon

JULY 7, 2021
Williams to Peoria, Arizona
172 miles

The day started out at a balmy 80 degrees when we had breakfast in Williams, Arizona. We had a marvelous breakfast, my usual omelette with fruit, in a Greek restaurant "Jessica's", named after the owner's daughter. The owner came out and talked with us, as he is also a motorcycle rider. We learned that he immigrated to the United States from Greece as a boy, initially settled in the Chicago area. He came here to the town of Williams as a young man and his restaurant is a fixture in downtown on Route 66.

We were headed south through Phoenix to Marana, Arizona. The further south we rode, out of the mountains and into the desert, the more burdensome the heat became. We left Williams, situated in the mountains, and slowly started towards lower elevation. Williams is at 6700 feet elevation but Phoenix is just over 1000 feet. Way off in the distance we saw the smoke of a forest fire. It was not totally out of control yet but we saw fire-fighting activity along the way. The terrain finally gave way to a sea of Saguaro cactus. The temperatures continued to rise drastically, and it reached a grievous 110 degrees today. I wonder what we have done to the environment to make it so angry with us?

However, I experienced all of this ride southbound in the air-conditioned cab of a wrecker with my Spyder motorcycle on the flatbed! The driver was a young guy who was articulate, intelligent and absolutely filthy. The truck was just purchased the week before and already had over 2000 miles on it. He was happy to fill me in on the surroundings and the fire and the names of cacti.

This morning after breakfast, we were eager to leave town for the days ride, when the parking brake on my bike locked up and would not release, no matter what I did. The manual said "call a dealer". After several calls I found a certified dealer in Peoria, Arizona, a suburb of Phoenix. They said they would work on it as soon as I could get it there. The police department was across the parking lot and they gave me the name of two reputable wrecker companies. I found this young fellow that was willing to take me 170 miles one way, immediately. To the tune of $1300! In spite of my detailed and avid preparations for this trip I missed getting a rider on my insurance policy for towing and/or delay of the trip.

Jackie was excited to visit her friend Joanne Bumstead, whom she had not seen in a couple of years. We both foolishly thought that after the 170-mile trip, the bike would be fixed in short order, we would still be in Marana by nightfall. While we waited nearly two hours for the wrecker, Jackie had great fun teasing me about the breakdown.

So finally, about noon, my bike was loaded on the wrecker and we were on our way with Jackie following to start. She took pictures of my bike before and after it was loaded on the flatbed. Why did we not put Jackie's bike on the wrecker too, and both ride inside in the cool air? Well, if you have a perfectly working bike you ride it, not tow it. The whole point is to ride the machine. Putting Jackie's bike on the flatbed was never a consideration. In hind sight, this heat could have caused Jackie her life.

We didn't go far and landed in backed up traffic outside of Flagstaff. The temperature was a stifling 100 degrees already. Once we finally got clear of the construction, moving about 75 mph, Jackie said the heat was not quite so bad. She drove into a rest stop while we kept going in the wrecker, arriving at the "Ride Now" dealership in Peoria about 3pm. They carried every make of motorcycle there is, except Harley Davidson.

I made myself comfortable in the large waiting area in the air conditioning, waiting for the diagnosis on my bike. Finally, by 4:30pm they gave me the news that the needed part was not in stock but they will have it Friday morning. Since the part and labor are under warranty, I just have to pay the priority shipping and of course the tow bill. The parking brake issue had started a couple days previous, but just briefly, and would eventually release on its own. This problem was known to BRP, the manufacturer of CanAm. They had switched manufacturers of the brake part, but my bike had not had the corrected part put on it.

In the meantime, while driving, I had talked to Jackie several times, but felt terrible when she turned off into a rest stop and was no longer in sight behind me. Anxiety at its highest. I'm not sure if my tears were for worrying about her, or the cost of this tow, or feeling sorry for myself that I was not out there riding with her, or a combination of all of it. The driver was courteous enough to leave me alone in my sorrow for a few minutes until I got past all of that. I had given Jackie the exit numbers along the way and the exact directions. She said she was stopping to pour her cold water on her head more than once. I was expecting her to cruise into the dealership any minute.

As I was getting the bad news on my bike, I got a text from her that said "I'm close but cannot make it any further". I called her right away, she said she was in a building and had to go to sleep, hung up on me. I immediately started looking for a hotel close by. The guys at the dealership were helpful and the mechanic helped me find a hotel that was fairly close. As I am on the phone on hold, making the reservation, Jackie is calling me and I can't answer her. . . I have no clue where she is but I was sure that she was suffering from heat exhaustion.

Jackie had followed my directions. She was within three blocks of the dealership when she became disoriented. Apparently, she stopped in front of a repair garage, put her head on her arms to rest. A very kind man came out and saved her, encouraging her to come inside their building to cool down. That's where she sent me the text of "I'm close", but after a few minutes in the cool air of the garage she felt better. They drew directions on a paper for her that she was unable to follow, but she did find the dealership by accident and got the bike parked and herself inside.

As soon as I could, I called her, she said she was in the building of the dealership now. The place is huge with several entrances, but I found her semi-conscious sitting in a chair just inside the door at the service entry, half laying across a table. I got her to drink my Essentia Water, replacing the electrolytes in her system. She perked up fairly quickly but really needed to be in cooler temps, get her whole body cooled down. The mechanic offered to drive us to the hotel, so we unloaded our stuff into his car. Jackie was alert enough to move her bike inside this building for the night but she was not in any shape to drive it any further. We were quite naïve to this grievous heat, what it could do to us, what the body can and cannot endure.

Once we arrived at the hotel Jackie continued to drink liquids and rest in the air conditioning. I ordered take-out food from a nearby restaurant for us. I walked in the heat about a quarter mile to pick it up. Once I returned to the hotel, we found that it was the wrong order, so I had to walk back to the restaurant a second time, in the heat, to get the right order. It would have been a nice walk, except the heat made it intolerable. We are quite disappointed to not see Joanne, but realize that it is not possible to ride further south to Marana, Arizona, in this onerous heat. I did not get to ride two miles today in this gorgeous state that is so foreign to me. With a day and half delay in our travels, we will leave here on Friday and go directly to Las Vegas, NV.

The irony of being stuck in Peoria, Arizona is that in the fall of 2017 Frankie and I had ridden out to South Dakota on my first Spyder, pulling the trailer. On the way back we broke down and had to wait in Peoria, Illinois for four days over a holiday weekend. I think Peoria of any state needs to be far away from my agenda.

7-7-21 Fire in the Mountains of Arizona

7-7-21 Nancy's Bike on the Wrecker

7-7-21 Saguaro cactus

JULY 8, 2021
Our day in Peoria, Arizona
0 miles

Today was going to be a rest day, a welcome recovery from the oppressive heat. We were going to relax and sit around the pool waiting until tomorrow to pick up my bike and get back on the road. Jackie and I decided to walk to the Harley-Davidson dealer, just one block from our hotel, to look for a new helmet for her. As we walked in the front door she forgot about the helmet because the first thing we saw was this eye popping burgundy and red H-D trike motorcycle. The misery of the day before, the tremendous heat, my fear of her heat exhaustion, was translated into this moment when we both looked at each other and said "trade in".

After around the second day of this trip Jackie started talking about having a Stage 2 put on her bike to give it more power. She found that she was having trouble keeping up on the freeway at higher speeds, especially in the foothills and the mountains. The heat coming off the motor was tremendous as it is not liquid cooled, and it certainly contributed to her heat exhaustion yesterday. Because of the heat from the motor and the exhaust, she always has to wear jeans to protect her skin from being burned. Also, she does not have any navigation system on the bike, other than a compass. Moreover, she is directionally challenged.

This beauty is a shiny 2017 Harley-Davidson Ultra Classic Trike with only 18,000 miles. It was obviously very well taken care of. It was like it was made for her, like she had to go through the suffering of yesterday in order to get to it. It had a liquid cooled engine to keep her legs from burning. The extra power of the engine will give her the ability to fly by me in the mountains. The computer and navigation system will give her a whole new world to experience. Jackie loves the black of the Harley, but these red colors together with the leather and the chrome, were like a gift she could not resist.

She eagerly started negotiating with the salesman, even though her old bike was still at the other dealership and not there for a trade-in. She showed them pictures of her delinquent bike. During this whole process her salesman drove us over to Ride Now to get her old bike and bring it here. In talking to the finance manager, she learned that he was originally from our part of Michigan and actually knows Ray C, of our local H-D dealership. They agreed on a trade-in value including moving her phone and cup holders to the new bike, along with adding new highway pegs and a new driver backrest. Jackie could not resist . . . Six wonderful hours later she rode it out the door. She came to the dealership to buy a helmet, drove out with a new bike and a free new helmet.

Jackie is jubilant with her new gift. Her elation is contagious. What a difference we feel tonight, hopeful and eager, compared to last nights' exhaustion and disappointment of my bike breakdown. We are now keenly awaiting tomorrow, to battle the heat and make our way to Las Vegas, Nevada.

7-8-21 Jackie's new bike

JULY 9, 2021
Peoria, Arizona to Las Vegas, Nevada
326 miles

We woke up this morning, ready for the challenge: we knew that today we had a long, extremely hot ride to Las Vegas. In the morning it was already in the mid 90's, and expected to hit 114 before the day was done. We believed that both of our bikes would be fine in this heat, as now they are both liquid cooled. To protect from the sun, I wore a UV protection long sleeve shirt and my usual capris. Jackie wore her black jeans along with a long sleeve, cotton Harley shirt. We stocked up on everything needed for the day's ride, extra water, Essentia water, ice and sandwich stuff in the cooler. We hoped that these supplies would get us through the tormenting heat of the day.

In the meantime, we counted on the fact that my bike would be fixed and ready to go by noon. I rode with Jackie back to the Ride Now dealership. Thankfully the parking brake had arrived but we had to wait for the installation. Finally, at 2:20pm I got my bike back, rode back to the hotel to load up; we ate a quick sandwich and were on our way by 3pm. By this time, it was 114 degrees. It felt like riding in an oven. The sweltering heat was now oppressive. We believed that once we got out of town, hit Hwy 60 and got up to cruising speed, the wind from our speed would make it tolerable to be in that heat.

It was about a 15-minute drive on a five-lane street to get to Hwy 60. At 10 minutes out, we stopped for Jackie to put cold cloths on her thighs. She was wearing black jeans that were soaking up the sun to the point of burning her skin. We hit Hwy 60, which is a four-lane divided highway running northwest towards Las Vegas. We had to stop in the shade of the first overpass to pour water on Jackie's head. I knew this was not going to be sustainable, but at this point I was okay myself. The next stop was five miles further, off on a blacktop 2-lane with half a shoulder width of gravel, with NO shade anywhere. Jackie was unable to go any farther, she is suffering from heat exhaustion again. She gave it her best, but she just could not ride in this heat and these clothes.

So, I'm helping Jackie get some Essentia water down and a little food. She started to perk back up and I was fine. Then, in the twinkling of an eye, something happened to my equilibrium. All of a sudden, I started to feel light headed as well, close to fainting, in a matter of about a minute. The only shade was from my bike, if I sat on my running board. Obviously, the electrolyte replacement was not enough. If we didn't get out of this furnace quickly, we would be in big trouble. I asked Jackie to wave somebody down. Luckily the first car was three guys coming from a nearby golf course. They kindly offered us their air-conditioned SUV for us to recover. We all clambered in, with one guy laying in the back with their golf bags. They offered us more cold water. Within 10 minutes we were both cooled down enough to go find some shelter from this 114-degree sun. It was like a breathing furnace that we have to get out of. But go where? Just up the road was the town of Wittmann, about 3 miles or so. We decided to go there for shelter, to escape the sun, wait until dark and ride to Vegas at night.

We turned right from Hwy 60 to a very small part of the small town of Wittmann, which was separated by the highway. We should have turned left, crossed the divide, and into the main town, but I think my semi-conscious brain turned the wrong way. Our first stop was next to a small church under shade of a scrappy little tree. We sat on a couple of cement blocks that I dragged over. This spindly little tree and its small patch of shade, even with the breeze from the desert, definitely was not our salvation. We were desperate to do better, we needed to be inside, in air conditioning, someplace real soon, or we would not make it until night fall.

There was a railroad track paralleling the highway where a very long, slow train was coming along, blocking the road to the main part of Wittmann. We stayed under that spindly little tree for about 20 minutes, isolated and alone, until the train finally cleared the highway so that we could cross. I seemed to be moving in slow motion as we crossed the train track and highway, headed for the ever-present Dollar General. On the way, I spotted the Post Office up ahead, with welcoming solid shade from the building on the parking lot. It's a public building, it should be open, and it should be air conditioned. It was like the Gods were looking over us, and we sped right up to the front and parked.

Now it's 4:45pm. We have come a grueling 25 miles in an hour and a half. The Post Office closed at 4:30pm but the lobby was open around the clock for the boxes and yes, it was air conditioned! So, we hauled the cooler in, thankful we were alive, a little worse for wear and sat on the floor to recover, wait for the welcome darkness. A United States Post Office never felt so good. There was one wall plug that we used to charge our phones as we sat on the floor. It didn't matter that there were no chairs. We thankfully found a place to shelter and recover. We were out of the sun's fiery breath.

This blessed little one-horse town had a busy Post Office. We were there about three and a half hours, at least 40 people came in for their mail. Some folks spoke and some did not. Some wanted to chat and some were quite skeptical of these two women escaping the sun, hanging out in their Post Office. One guy said that we were making good use of our tax dollars! There was a party store across the street so we individually walked over there for snacks and ice cream. They did not have a public bathroom, so we had to improvise. The back side of the building worked just fine but I was wide-eyed for snakes.

While sitting there in the post office, so thankful in the cool air, I saw a scrawny, chicken-like bird scrabbling around outside in the gravel and weeds. She was fun to watch with her bushy blue-black crest and mottled plumage among the gravel. How interesting and hope inspiring that this seldom seen and underappreciated roadrunner would come to visit us in our near disaster. I was mesmerized by the energy this bird had in this stifling heat. This roadrunner, revered for their "courage, strength, speed, and endurance" gave us the courage to face the night ahead, of riding in the dark of the dessert while the sun is gone to rest.

Of course, we were watching the weather and there was a significant thunderstorm coming in around 6:30pm, temperatures were showing to be in the high 80s just after the storm at 8pm. So that was our target to leave for Las Vegas. Except the sun got the best of it, the storm broke up and the temperatures did not drop. It has become paramount that we ride when the sun is down. We knew that as long as the sun was asleep, we could make it to Las Vegas in the dark overnight.

It was 8:10pm and the sun with its fiery breath was finally down. It was still hot, but not like it was earlier, probably closer to 110. It was time for us to say goodbye to our shelter in the Post Office. My bike GPS would not pick up Angie Gutierrez's address in Vegas for whatever reason, but we knew it was a straight shot northwest across the desert. I have our routes all typed out on nice 4x6 inch cards that fit on my safety card that fits nicely inside my dashboard. Except I can't read these nice directions in the dark! So, our navigation was the GPS mapping only and my instincts. And it was very dark. All cloud cover, no stars or moon to see. Dark is Dark. No stars, no moon, no glows from the towns, no nothing. Just white and yellow lines on a black strip, mile after mile. I could not tell if we were in the desert or the forest. The traffic was light, which was welcome, but again that much less light for us.

The temperatures were as high as 114 and as low as 88 for one brief mile as we rode through the night. Mostly it was between 100 and 110 degrees. We kept our golf neck scarves wet from the ice water in the cooler, which lasted about an hour each time, and really did help keep our heads clear. What would have been a beautiful 270-mile ride, turned into 326 HOT miles in the dark. Apparently at Wickenburg we zigged instead of zagged and about 20 miles later I realized we were going southwest instead of northwest. We both checked our phone GPS and they both directed us over to 95, taking us into the edge of California through the towns of Needles and Parker and God only knows where else. This route added about 56 miles which normally would not be a problem, but definitely not welcome this night.

We stopped a few times to replenish our water and twice to have a little cool-down in party stores. At one town just into California we stopped at a well-lit party store, went in to get something cold to eat, cool down in the air conditioning for a few minutes. The temperature was still hovering around 95 to 100 degrees. As I looked around, I could see that we were not in a good area, I didn't feel good leaving the bikes unattended. Usually, one or the other of us stayed with the bikes. So I kept going in and out, slowly eating my ice cream, watching the bikes but still trying to cool myself down inside the store. Sure enough, a car load of fine fellows scrutinizing the bikes needed watching. I would not leave them alone and they finally left.

Some of the gas stations were closed but we could buy gas with a credit card. All of their outside lights were on, the pumps lit up, but the store was closed. The last fill at 1:30am somewhere, would not accept either of my debit cards or credit card. I think we were still in California. I appreciate the security involved in using these cards; I had contacted all cards ahead, listing the states we would be in, but security still prevailed. Fortunately for me, Jackie's card worked fine so she covered my fill-up.

It was a long, strange night of wakefulness, trying to beat the sun's waking up. We were bone tired when we stopped at the welcome sight of an all-night casino, the parking lot lit up like day-time. We each went inside to use the facilities, with its flashing lights and the jingle jangle of slot machines, giving us a reprieve from the dark, hot night. I put Angie's address into the GPS again, this time we knew she was only 50 more miles up the road. The last hour I talked to Jackie continuously and nonsensically to keep of us both awake and our eyes wide open in the darkness. We arrived here at Angie Gutierrez's home at 3am, having taken seven hours total, instead of four. Thankfully, we made it to Las Vegas safe and sound, riding like Roadrunners through the darkness of the desert with no stars and no moon, just white and yellow lines on a black strip.

7-9-21 Jackie ready to go on the new bike

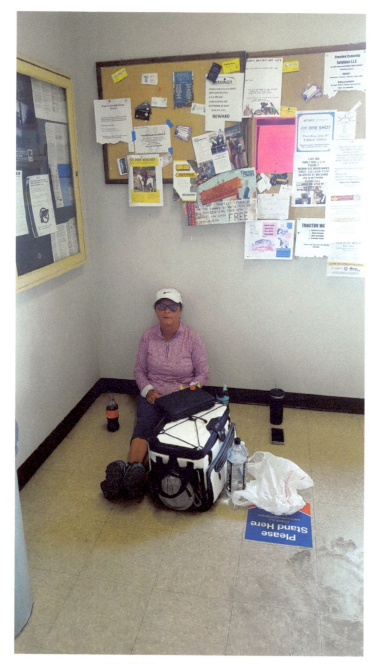

7-9-21 Nancy in Post Office

7-9-21 Roadrunner

JULY 10, 2021
Las Vegas, Nevada - A day to rest and recover

After just a few hours of sleep, I woke up thankful to have arrived and to be in Angie's home. Her two-bedroom, two-bath apartment on the ground floor is part of a large gated complex. Her parking lot with the red painted curbing had a welcome appeal as the red stood out against the abundantly green landscaping, especially the large trees in full foliage. Normally I would be drawn to sit under the shade of the trees in a lawn chair, but the heat is too oppressive. Angie kindly gave us her covered parking spot for our bikes in front of her apartment, so she had to park her car in an open uncovered free spot, far away from her building. Just walking to her car from the apartment in this heat was tough and it was only mid-morning.

For lunch, we headed out in Angie's air-conditioned car, on the 40-mile drive to the Pioneer Saloon, at Goodsprings, Nevada to meet Dan & Marty Noltie and their families. They are the sons of Joanne, whom we did not get to visit in Marana, Arizona because of the bike breakdown. We drove through the dry, brown, rocky desert, a stark contrast to the neatly manicured, green landscaping of her complex. This view across the dessert, against the mountains in the background, is what we didn't see driving here through the dark of the night.

The Pioneer Saloon was built in 1913 and has been the site of several movies. Except for air conditioning, the décor had not been changed or upgraded since the beginning. The bar and tables are all original. The finish is gone, and the wood is old, scarred and smooth. The ceilings have the original tin squares as well. Eight of us sat around a big round table that had been reinforced underneath with 2x4's a long time ago. After the isolation and darkness of last night's ride, I relished the congeniality of visiting and laughing with new faces.

We returned to Las Vegas to the MGM Grand for a little gambling and dinner. I had my usual win a little – lose a little luck at the slots. I appreciated seeing the lights, the variety of people and the general commotion of the casino. Angie had promised us luxurious dinners on her comps and she did not disappoint. She led us to the International Woodfired Smoke restaurant. I had a scrumptious rack of baby back ribs served with full length uncut carrots.

All in all, we were thankful for this day of visitation and rest, even if we were cruising on just a couple hours of sleep. It was one of those days when you start laughing and can't stop, at something that really isn't that funny. What a difference of day and night, from one day to the next, riding out in the open, in overpowering heat and heavy isolation of darkness, to relaxing in an air-conditioned old-cowboy bar and then an elegant, classy restaurant, reveling in the gaiety of a Las Vegas casino.

7-10-21 Desert outside Las Vegas

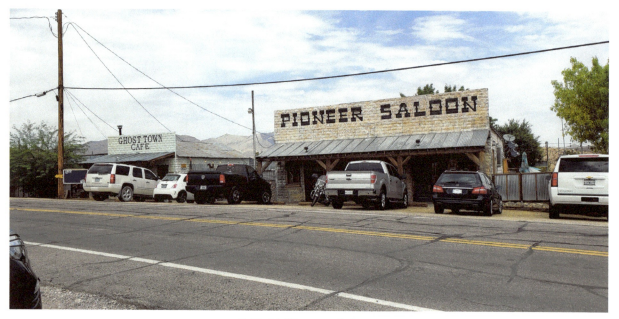

7-10-21 Pioneer Saloon

7-10-21. Us at Pioneer Saloon

JULY 11, 2021
A relaxing day in Las Vegas
0 miles

We had been on the road for 10 days so we were happy to settle into the needed rest and relaxation here in Vegas. I am a breakfast eater, whereas Jackie and Angie are not. I debated riding my bike to the grocery store, about a mile away, but it was 115 degrees outside, so I would have been roasted by the time I arrived there. I was glad for Angie's offer of her car along with good directions, and easily located a grocery store for the needed eggs and such. Jackie's new helmet needed a little more work on the installation of the intercom system and some extra cushion for her hard head, so the second order of business was to collect the needed supplies for that project. My helmet needed a little extra padding too, so we got both helmets fixed and adjusted and are ready for more adventures in a couple of days.

Then we drove the length of the Strip in air-conditioning, with Jackie and Angie reminiscing about previous trips here and all of the changes. The last time I was here was in about 2008, when everything was free and open. Today everything feels closed in, with the walls and barriers blocking the street from the sidewalks and buildings. Either shrubbery, metal framework, or cement abutments, all about waist high, are constructed to be aesthetically pleasing to the eye, but confining the person for safety. Today it is necessary to protect us from those who will do harm: to keep the jaywalkers out of the street or vehicles from driving into the crowds on the sidewalk, or right into a building. It was the tragedy of the shooter that took so many lives at the concert in 2017 that was the beginning of this lack of trust and freedom.

It was truly astounding to me, that there were so many people on the street, here on the Strip, in this 115-degree heat. We saw a few people that were clearly suffering and being assisted by others. Hopefully they were just moving from building to building, but that distance of several blocks in this heat is dangerous. Other than directly on the strip, I didn't see anyone outside doing anything. No people walking dogs, no kids playing anything, including sports. Every park and playground we passed was empty. Excruciating sun has robbed folks of delighting in its presence. Everyone goes out early in the morning or after dark in order to avoid the piercing rays of the sun. Being from Michigan, I have never experienced this kind of overpowering heat. I was always under the impression that when the heat is dry like this, rather than muggy, that we would feel comfortable in it. It's like the sun is becoming an enemy.

Tonight, Angie took us to another of her favorite gambling spots, the Belagio, famed for its elegance. The ceiling in the lobby, over 2000 multi-colored glass flowers moving in the breeze, are so delicate they look weightless, like paper. Furthermore, Belagio's conservatory and botanical gardens along with the dancing water fountain display, leaves one astonished. An Italian restaurant, Lago, was our choice for dinner. The seating area was long and narrow, next to the glass wall separating us from the open main walkway and the casino. My meal was an exquisite chicken dish; the gambling, not quite so exquisite for me, but the casino crowds were magnificent. As part of this social scene, we were relaxed, happy and full.

7-11-21 Belagio glass ceiling

7-11-21 Front of Restaurant

JULY 12, 2021
Another day in Las Vegas
0 miles

Our motorcycles were patiently waiting outside under the cover of the parking spot, but the temperatures remain in the 117-degree range, oppressive and unwelcoming. I had wanted to go out and visit the Hoover Dam but it was just too hot. I was there in 2008 and was struck by its immense size, looming 726 feet over the Black Canyon. The dam spans the Colorado River, thereby developing Lake Meade, which is the largest reservoir in the United States. Hoover Dam provides electricity to Nevada, Arizona and California. Lake Meade is the main water source to Arizona, California, Colorado, Nevada, New Mexico, Utah and Wyoming. The water level has been decreasing slowly since 2000, bringing the present level now to less than 50 percent, all due to drought. The trip out to Hoover Dam and a visit to the Zion National Park in Utah will wait for a future trip.

I cannot WAIT to get back on the road Wednesday morning. Instead, we continued another day visiting around Las Vegas. First, Angie took us to the world-famous Gold & Silver Pawn Shop where the reality show is filmed. It is very small compared to what folks see on TV, not more than 2000 square feet. I had fun looking at all of the jewelry, but nothing was appealing enough for me to make a purchase.

Then we went downtown to the Plaza Hotel and Casino, out onto the Fremont Experience, a pedestrian mall that stretches for five blocks on Fremont Street. A canopied light show stretches between the building tops, spectacular and easily seen in the daytime. There was plenty of live music on the street as we wandered in and out of the small casinos, restaurants and gadget stores along the way. Most businesses had cool air blowing from machine's sitting outside, and their doors wide open. This was the only place in Las Vegas that we found we could be comfortable being outside in the daytime in the piercing rays of the sun, due to the shade of the canopy. The homeless were quite prevalent on Fremont Street because it was cooler. Some were trying to sell some little thing, or juggling, or trying to keep busy so they could earn their spot on the street and not get shooed away. Later in the trip we saw huge amounts of homeless in northern California, Oregon and Washington. I am wondering if the homeless migrate further north to escape this unbearable heat in the summertime.

We returned to the MGM Grand where Angie treated us again with her compensations. We chose Wolfgang Puck and it was worth the hour wait. The hot-wing appetizers were more candied, as opposed to spicy hot. The chicken meal that I ordered was delicious. Shortly after we were seated a man asked to join us, as there was no place else for him to sit. Seated at a long table along the back wall, we three had all sat on one side, facing the crowd. We were surprised because we found that most people were courteous but distant, preferring to remain in the safety of their own self and immediate friends. He sat on the other side, facing us and chatting pleasantly, but once our food arrived, he over-stepped his bounds, attempted to take some food off Angie's plate. The restaurant staff courteously removed him from our table, as we finished another fun day in Las Vegas.

7-12-21 Fremont St Roof

7-12-21 Fremont Street Light Show

JULY 13, 2021
Our last day in Las Vegas
0 miles

We were eager to get back on the road, but today the temperatures are still at 115 degrees. We are hoping it will be better tomorrow. Today we did laundry and picked up supplies, especially water for back on the road tomorrow. I spotted a small Windmill water stand in the middle of a parking lot. They were selling dispensed water at $1.50 for a gallon and $5 for three gallons. It was a stand-alone building, not manned by anyone, just a dispenser on each side so you could bring your own jugs to fill. This small windmill water stand reminds me of how thankful we are that water is ample and plentiful for us to obtain, especially in this heat.

Angie wanted us to have one final fling at the MGM although I had enough of gambling. I am ready for the open road. She wanted us to have one last free, luxurious meal. We were thankful for all of the indescribable meals that she shared with us. As we eat our faithful sandwich in the coming days we will remember.

This evening we are reorganizing and packing for an early morning exit from Vegas tomorrow. Eagerly awaiting cooler temperatures. Four days away from my bike seems too long, about two too many on this trip. In order to survive in this heat, we have had to alter our trip. We can no longer take the planned trip into Utah and the national parks. And the two-day trip to San Diego to see my niece Rachel and her husband Alan is not possible. I was eagerly looking forward to seeing them, especially their new son Anders who turned one in June. In the bottom of my orange dry bag is a birthday present, a book, to give to him. In spite of my disappointment, I can take comfort in the fact that they will be in Michigan in September when I am back. It will be a book with a lot of miles inside it. In working on my quest to visit all of the states, I hope to plan another future trip out here to catch Utah, Texas, Oklahoma, and Arkansas, completing all states west of the Mississippi.

7-13-21 Windmill Water Dispenser

JULY 14, 2021
Las Vegas to Reno, Nevada
454 miles

The bikes were waiting patiently to be off in spite of the heat, ready for another new adventure. It's good to be back in the saddle. Las Vegas has little to offer when I can be on the road, free and easy, watching the miles disappear under us. It was a beautiful 85 degrees when we left Vegas this morning just after 7am, and remained under 90 for the first three hours. We took the 215 west around the city, then headed northwest into the desert on I-95 towards Reno. We relished the green trees and shrubbery only found in the towns as we passed through.

As we traveled along there was nothing but brown and gray prairies with mountains in the distance. The shades of brown were varied and fascinating, some of the mountains reminded me of the pink tan colored uniform pants that I wore for 10 years of my law enforcement career. They were a light brown with a bit of a pink tan shade to them, "pink tan" was the real name of the pants color. I hate brown to this day and avoid it as much as possible in relation to clothes. After about 4 hours of riding in the desert, we both decided that in Michigan, the protection of surrounding green, woods and fields in full bloom, is more pleasing to our eyes. Maybe brown is the new color of this global crisis we are in. Nothing can grow and the earth is scorched.

For a little shade, we pulled into Beaty, Nevada, a town out of the old wild west with dirt streets and wooden walkways, the only pavement being the two-lane black strip of Highway 95 running through the town. It was natural that we were welcomed by a group of wild burros. The shade of the only tree to be seen was taken up by a wild burro, all of his friends and family close by. As we approached the tree on our bikes, he was unafraid of our invasion of his space. It was like he belonged there, in the desert in the middle of this little town. He courteously gave up the shade and wandered over, led the pack as they ambled across the road, stopping all traffic on Highway 95.

Hwy 95 in Nevada is primarily a two-lane strip of pavement running north and south through the desert and between the mountain ranges. There was absolutely nothing between the towns. No pastures, no farms, no settlements in the distance, no nothing. Just immediate desert and mountains in the distance. Vehicle speeds seemed to be unchecked, but we remained around 70mph. We stopped in the town of Tonopah to eat our sandwiches next to the Tonopah Station building. We shared the shadow patch and refreshing bit of breeze, with a young family having a picnic out of the back seat of their car. As we continued north the foothills changed over to buttes and the higher elevations of the mountains, but the colors remained the same seared brown. We rode for several miles along Walker Lake with the mountains close on our left. Against the parched desert and mountains, the welcome blues of the water made these views the most beautiful part of the day.

After riding across miles of desert, over the foothills with the buttes and mountains in the distance, the small towns were always a gleeful sight of civilization. We drove through two different towns with small military bases on the outskirts, the people busily engaging in everyday life, coming and going. But there were other towns that were dead. The town of Goldfield was one such place. It clearly had been upgraded at some point to look like a cowboy town out of the 1800's or so. But today every business was closed, buildings were run down, the people had disappeared. It was like driving through an abandoned ghost town. However, it appears that the population is about 200 people and it has tours of the old, ghost ridden hotel.

Thirty miles further we passed through a town that advertised itself as being RV "friendly". The friendly part of the town only pertained to the RV park that was occupied with RV's. The town itself was dead. The buildings were falling down, burned out, or in such disrepair that they just looked rat infested. Jackie was looking for ice cream in this heat. We saw a modern sign for an ice cream shop that was the only place not in disrepair. We stopped, but it too was abandoned, just like the rest of the town. I saw a man standing in a dark doorway of an abandoned building and I waved. He waved back.

As we traveled north through the desert, the temperatures began to rise.

We started out at 85 degrees and it kept rising as the day wore on. The last couple hours of riding were in the 101 to 105 range. Between the two of us we drank 100 ounces of Essentia water along with just as much regular water and ice. We regularly dipped our neck scarves in the melting ice of the cooler to keep the heat tolerable. The few times that we stopped we cherished what little shade we could find. The need for constant fluids was overwhelming. In one little military town an hour outside of Reno we stopped for gas and rested a little in air conditioning. I will always remember the frozen Chocolate Peanut Butter Protein Smoothie, mixed in a machine. It was a first for me and surely not my last. That got me into Reno.

To my surprise, as we were approaching Reno, traveling on a two-lane in an industrial area, we saw a herd of wild horses standing in the shade of the back side of a large Wal-Mart warehouse. We felt an affinity with the wild burros and the wild horses seeking shade in the desert. Thankfully, we easily found our hotel, the Circus-Circus casino. We were so happy to pull into the shade of the underground registration area and stopped. Since we were beat, hot and tired, we immediately took off our helmets and got out our purses. The bellhop then told us that we had to move the bikes into the other lane, by just riding back out onto the street, around the loop and back in against the curb. We moved the bikes and then unloaded completely onto their little cart. Then as directed, we drove the bikes across the street and into the parking ramp, parked, locked up.

AND . . . . Jackie's wallet is missing! She had it out initially because she was going to register upon arrival. It was literally nowhere to be found. So, of course we back tracked on the street and the parking ramp, checked with the bellhop, checked with security, with no luck. Now Jackie is hot, and just short of panicking. This hotel is in her name and paid for, so she was in line to register in spite of having no wallet, no id, no credit card, and no confirmation number. In the meantime, I went back to the bellhop station and our cart of luggage to retrieve her notebook with the confirmation in it. The cart had been locked into a back room so I had to wait for an escort to retrieve the notebook. When I returned to the counter, I could see that Jackie is failing fast, profuse sweating, going into heat exhaustion. The clerk has now turned her over to a manager, both of them not letting her register. I realize I have to move fast, so I go back again to the bellhop, got an escort to our luggage cart, go through my dry bag searching for a bottle of Essentia water that she seriously needs. I can't find it. So, I opened the cooler to at least get her another bottle of cold water. There is her wallet . . . in the cooler!

After 450 miles in the hot desert, this room in this hotel was like luxury. I realize that the gods were looking over us, because I would not have found Jackie's wallet if I had found the Essentia water in the dry bag the first time I looked. How would we have ever arrived in this room without her wallet? I found the Essentia water in my dry bag, where it belonged, once we were in the room. We arrived at the hotel at 3:30pm when the temperatures were not even at their peak, but the heat and exhaustion that occurred is serious. 100 ounces of Essentia water plus at least that much regular water between the two of us, and we still need more. It took a while for Jackie to get properly hydrated and cooled down in the air-conditioned room. I too was in need of fluids and to get a body cool-down, I took a cool shower to get back to normal. After a good night's sleep, we intend to slay our dragon, the sun. Tomorrow will see if we are successful.

7-14-21 Burrows in town on the road

7-14-21 Walker Lake

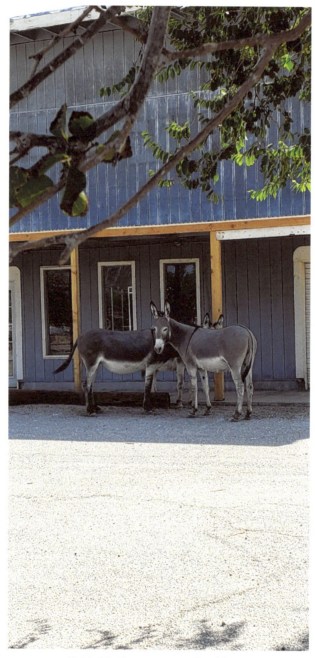

7-14-21. Burros near building

JULY 15, 2021
Reno, Nevada to Arcata, California
372 miles

The route that I had planned for today was going to take us north out of Reno, west through the Sierra Nevada mountains, through Greenville, and over to Redding, California. As I pulled the maps up on my phone, across the top was a red ribbon running, warning of fires. Also, little red and yellow tongues of fire in the mountains on the map warning us that we had to change our route. These tongues were the Dixie fire that started on July 13, eventually becoming the 2nd largest fire recorded in California, burning almost a million acres, and not contained until the end of October. The drought, combined with hot weather, strong winds and exceptionally dry vegetation fed this fire. Whether they are set by man or nature, fire fighters are unable to stop the fires because of the lack of moisture, the winds and the acute dryness.

We changed our route to travel southwest on I-80, then west on Hwy 174 and 20. We will turn north on Highway 70 all the way into Redding. We left at 8am with comfortable, cooler temperatures in the low 70's, wearing jackets for the first time since we left Michigan. Shortly after leaving Reno, we could see smoke in the distance to the north, but never smelled it. We rode through the north edge of the Tahoe National Forest, relishing the fact that the dry brown desert of the last few days is now behind us. The scenic views of the deep green, dense evergreen forests surround us. We are basking in the shade everywhere. Our first stop at a rest area allowed us to see across the tops of trees, down into a deep valley with a river at the bottom. Every tree, bush, shrub and scrub were a lush green, except for the grass which was yellow, an indicator of dire drought. I could see how a forest fire would be devastating and nearly impossible to stop.

After leaving the freeway with its green spectacular of the mountains, we traveled on 2-lane roads that took us through fields of orange groves and other fruits, that stretched for miles and miles around us. Riding on the two-lane roads is by far my favorite way to travel. I just seem to soak up my surroundings. We made a game of identifying what fruit was being grown as we traveled past them, but for the most part we did not know. We decided that there needs to be signage to tell us tourists what's what. The sweet smell of the orange groves, with their uplifting orange fruit, filled us with excitement and a sense of adventure.

The sense of adventure soon got us into another event with another fool hardy driver. We turned north onto Highway 70 with heavy southbound truck traffic and only half a shoulder width. The thought entered my mind that this was a good spot for somebody to be passing the slow-moving trucks. Sure enough, in about a mile somebody swung out to pass, head-on at us. In a split-second reaction, I got my bike slowed down to 30mph, off onto the shoulder as far as I could. He flew by me, just pulling into his lane as he passed. Initially I yelled so Jackie had time to get out of the way. This was our third time to avoid a near-miss with a fool.

We finally had to get back on the freeway, I-5, at Red Bluffs, and took that up into Redding. As we got into Redding the temperatures rose to 97 degrees. Prior to that there had been a steady rise in the temperatures, but stayed very comfortable. We took CA299 west from Redding, 147 miles all the way to CA101, the Pacific coast road. Within a mile of leaving Redding, we could see the devastation of a huge forest fire. Such a lost feeling, black sticks of charred trees, nothing but black on the ground, for as far as we could see, both sides, for miles. If we looked hard enough there was a whisper of a green whisker, the ground growth beginning.

This area burned last year, July of 2020. Amongst the burned-out foundations, we saw several homes that looked to be brand new, as well as temporary trailers on property with construction in progress. The global crisis is increasing while we watch. The drought, the heat on a rampage, is destroying spectacular parts of this country. We rode through the Whiskeytown-Shasta-Trinity National Recreation Area and along the huge Whiskeytown lake for many miles. By November 2021 the fires have consumed a lot of land along Willow Creek and surrounding areas, after we went through.

CA299 is a winding, curvy, up and down two-lane road that is filled with hope and adventure. It meanders through the mountains with passing lanes every 10 miles or so and turn-offs to let traffic by. We were comfortable riding about 45mph. The Trinity River and Willow Creek ran along beside us, mostly to our left, as we were on the north side of the river for most of the way. The first 50 miles of this was fun with spectacular views, although it was hot riding in the direct sunlight. Temperatures remained in the high 90's. The next 50 miles were not as spectacular since I was beginning to get a little tired of all of this. A 20-minute power nap is all I needed. We were drinking lots of water, Essentia water and protein bars. We were also wearing the cooling scarves dipped in the ice water of the cooler. Some shade of those cooling pine forests is really all we needed at this moment. We stopped in a rest area, I laid down on the seat of a cement table in the shade and closed my eyes. I slept for a few minutes and woke up ready to tackle the next 50 miles. I looked around, saw that there were a couple of electric car chargers in the parking lot, seemingly out of place in this vast forest of wilderness.

We continued following along the Willow River, around the curves, up the hills, down the sides of the mountain, still always in the sun. We have not slain our dragon yet. My hands hurt, my arms hurt, my shoulders hurt, my back hurts and this is no longer spectacular. I just want to put my feet in the cooling river that we are riding along. For a minute I wished my bike was a horse and I could dangle my feet in the water as we ride through it.

Near the town of Willow Creek, we crossed the river to the south side and into the heavenly shade of the forest and mountains. At a stand in Willow Creek, we got a hot dog, and I cashed in on the peach grove. Two peaches, sweet and succulent, in the dense forest. I ate one, juicy, sweet and cool going down. The other one I savored for later in the hotel. We got carried away talking with the sellers, and left town forgetting to fill our gas tanks. We reassured ourselves that we both should have enough gas to get to Arcata anyway, our destination in 47 miles. Then Jackie's low fuel light came on and she does not know how far this new bike will go. So, now she is busy trying to figure out how to handle the situation if she runs out of gas.

In the meantime, we felt a significant drop in the temperature as we approached the coast of the Pacific Ocean. We had crossed the river, were now riding on the southside, with almost total shade from the mountains. Most of the afternoon we had been traveling on the north side of the river with the sun directly beating on us. The temperatures were now doing a revolution, from savoring the coolness at first, within 10 minutes we were freezing. Before we could ride the 30 miles to the gas station in Blue Lake, we had to stop, each of us put on two coats and gloves. We got into the hotel about 6pm, the temperature was 58 degrees and overcast from the ocean. This is the first day I've worn a jacket since July 1st. We will be here for two days; the temperatures are supposed to be in the 60's the whole time. A welcome change from heat exhaustion. Yesterday we were drowning in 100 ounces of Essentia water, an air-conditioned room and cool showers. Today we arrive wearing two coats and gloves. I guess we slayed the dragon after all. The wonders of experiencing wind therapy.

7-15-21 Park with Electric Chargers

7-15-21 Mountains along river

7-15-21 Mountains

JULY 16, 2021
Shopping & Visit the Redwood National Forest
128 miles

We have arrived at the Pacific Ocean with its cooler temperatures, surrounded by the marvelous green everywhere. After several days of tolerating the brown heat of the desert, devastation of the fires and tremendous thirst, the smell of the ocean is alluring. Today we are going to celebrate this renewal, so totally opposite from yesterday, and engulf ourselves with the green of the vegetation and the blue of the ocean.

We started the day with breakfast at the Phoenix Café in Arcata that had their own organic vegetable and herb garden. Amidst the greenery of the surrounding garden and the scent of fresh herbs, we sat back and felt at home, savoring a delicious cup of coffee, joining other folks in the outdoor seating area. It seemed very Californian. The breeze from the ocean shore is drawing us to come and explore its vastness. We rode out around Arcata Bay on the barrier peninsula of Manila, looking for a place to dip our toes in the Pacific. The land was private so we could not get to the ocean from here. So, we decided to be patient with the ocean until later.

As we returned to the mainland of Eureka, crossing two bridges, Jackie exclaimed that there was an icon on her computer map showing a Harley store nearby. Jackie is drawn, like a bee to honey, to any Harley-Davidson store and now her new computer shows her where they are. She is ecstatic. She had fun adding to her Harley collection of clothes and stuff. Because of our change in temperatures, I needed a heaver pair of riding gloves. I found a pair that has a teeny tiny little H-D logo, that I will ignore. I quit wearing my half gloves with gel palms, on about the fourth day out because they were too hot. Now my hands have toughened up and I don't need any gloves, except for warmth. My other purchase at Harley-Davidson was a new bell for Jackie's new bike, a good luck charm for safe riding, to keep the demons away. A little bell with a little bling. She graciously accepted it and attached it to her framing in the parking lot.

We went on to Walmart because I realize that I don't have enough heavy clothes for these cooler temperatures. I left my chaps home because of space. I don't have any sweatshirts and only one pair of full socks. I have jeans and with the pants of my rainsuit my legs will be fine. A sweatshirt or two is on the agenda, after I find full socks. This Walmart was the most unorganized mess of a store that I have ever seen. Jackie wanted a bandana for a headband…$2 and it was locked up! Brand-name socks and underwear were also under lock and key. Apparently, the theft problem is huge and these kinds of items are the first choice. We went to Kohl's nearby and I got my needed socks for these cooler temperatures. Luckily, Essentia water was not under lock and key at Walmart so we were able to replenish our supply.

We are now ready to dip our toes in the ocean, so we got on Highway 101, that runs the whole length of the Pacific in the United States, and headed north. Within 15 miles we got off at Clam Beach, just north of Arcata, where there was public access. It was about 63 degrees by then and the tide was out. The breeze was cool so jackets were necessary. We sat on a large driftwood by the high grasses to take off our shoes and socks. The water was calm and cool, the variety of blue shades, from green blues to dark blues is always a wonder to me. Walking in the vast, flat water gave me a sense of peacefulness. The sand was surprisingly hot on my tender little soles, so the new socks and shoes were quickly back on after walking in the ocean. On my quest to ride my bike in all states and provinces in North America, I also intend to put my feet in both oceans, the Gulf of Mexico and all of the Great Lakes.

We rode north on 101 with continual staggering views. We would be driving along surrounded by huge trees with a full canopy above, smelling the woodsy smell, then come around a curve, breaking out into a magnificent view of the ocean and its flavor. Going from one very woodsy dirt smell immediately into the salt sand of the ocean is an enticing cocktail for my senses to process. We stopped at the visitor's center for the Redwood National Forest and were directed to the Newton B Drury Scenic Parkway that runs up through the park between Highway 101 and the ocean.

This Parkway was a slow, curvy paved road meandering through the dense redwoods. The coastal redwoods are the tallest living thing on earth. Towering above us, with little sunlight coming through, we rode our seemingly miniature bikes in solid shade for 10 miles, miraculously looking up all the way to the top of the 100+ foot trees. In a car you can only see out, but you cannot see up to the majesty of the towering heights. One feels so small, like a particle, surrounded by the grandeur and majestic serenity of these trees. The acute scent of redwood mixed with the overwhelming odor of dirt, enveloped us. This was not a musty smell, just a fascinating odor that has stuck with me. Going through the Redwoods was like a lesson in awe and inspiration, their sense of strength to withstand the winds, the heat, and the fire.

Leaving the Redwood Park, we headed back south on 101 towards Arcata.

We turned off into Patrick's Point and rode along a bluff just above the ocean. We soaked up the freedom of salt from the ocean mixed with the smell of the green foliage and wild flowers all around us. We found a turn-out, took a break to watch the water and the rocks below us. A young man pointed out dozens of seals on one big rock, soaking up the sun. Just past this spot was a location where part of the road had fallen away, but we were able to pass across on temporary gravel and ride further south.

We continued along this ocean side road, came into Trinidad where we found the Trinidad Eatery. While we waited to be seated for dinner, we took a walk to the edge of the bluff overlooking a large bay and marina. This was a popular place for happy tourists, along with a gift shop where I bought a sweatshirt to wear in these cool temperatures. It's hard to find a sweatshirt without a hood, but I did, and put it on right then as the evening temperatures were coming in. How easily I forgot the heat of yesterday, as I snuggled into the comfort of the sweatshirt.

Just like the Redwoods were a lesson in awe and inspiration, so too the Pacific Ocean with its shades of blue and green, depending on the angle. The smells of wet sand and salt, walking in the ocean gave me a cooling sense of adventure. On our way to the closest laundromat, just one mile in from all of that glorious beauty we arrived at a strip mall filled with a large encampment of people without homes. They seemed to be everywhere. They are allowed to park old campers right on the street and live out of them. All of their stuff is stacked around the camper. Clearly not being driven or pulled anywhere. Where they are they stay, in the small security of their possessions. There are encampments in the most unbelievable places. It was such an anthesis from all of the beauty and grandeur of the coast. Through the broken glass of the building we watched our bikes closely, not trusting the people of this encampment. What training teaches us to judge the homeless?

7-16-21 Particle in the Redwoods

7-16-21 Bikes in the Redwoods

7-16-21 Redwood Beauty

7-16-21 Redwoods

7-16-21. Nancy in Pacific Ocean

JULY 17, 2021
Arcata, California to Salem, ORregon
386 miles

Today we are looking forward to a cooler, much more comfortable ride along the Pacific Ocean all the way up into Oregon. We delayed our departure for an hour, waiting for the temperature to come up a little and the fog to lift. We headed out about 9:30am in a foggy, misty 56 degrees. We both had to layer up, I put on my rainsuit pants along with the new socks and my favorite new sweatshirt. I relished my new heavier gloves along with my heated handlebars. A dramatic change from two days previous when I was wearing a short sleeve UV shirt, capri pants and no socks.

We traveled north on Highway 101, the Pacific Coast Scenic Parkway, all the way to Newport, Oregon, nearly 300 miles. The fog cleared quickly and the temperatures soon began to rise into the mid 60's. We especially appreciated the first 40 miles since the wildness of the green forest had already enchanted us yesterday.

This Parkway varies from narrow two-lane pavement in the forest to five lanes through towns, to 4-lane divided, but no freeway. The road is winding, curving, up and down hills, right along beside the ocean. Sometimes we would be riding deep in the serenity of the very tall forest, when we would come around a curve to a blue and dazzling view of the ocean. Sometimes we were just several yards from the ocean's sandy edge, sometimes 100 feet above overlooking a rocky bluff. The experience of riding the Pacific coast was beyond my wildest expectations.

As we crossed the border into Oregon, we were met with three signs. The very first sign startled me. It read "Cannabis for Sale." A mile up the road the second sign welcomed us. It read "Oregon Welcomes You". Then about a mile later we were met with the third sign that could raise fear in anyone. It said "Tsunami Hazard Zone"! I wasn't sure I read that right, but sure enough in about two miles, the same sign repeated itself, all the way up the Oregon coast. It further said "In case of earthquake go to higher ground or inland." Of course, the northwest United States, Canada and Alaska are prone to earthquakes or volcanos that could cause a tsunami. Here we are, having come through exhaustion from the deadly heat, avoided forest fires, three near-miss traffic accidents, and now we are being warned of a tsunami? Well, the thought entered my mind that I sure hope we don't have one of those today. Ponder this thought for a minute, the placement of the signs: Cannabis is the comfort sign that welcomes us to Oregon and prepares us for the fear of a tsunami disaster?

Around noon we stopped for lunch at Harris Beach, way up on a bluff, one of many small parks along the ocean. A lady coming up from a trail down to the beach said it was two tenths of a mile down. We made our sandwiches on the seat of Jackie's bike, then sat on a bench at the edge of the bluff, overlooking the peaceful blue of the ocean, a welcome sight after our trio of signs experience.

Of course, I was going to take advantage of the exercise to get to the water, so down I went. The trail was a narrow, switchback, steep gravel footpath just wide enough for one person. The path alone was worth the walk. At the bottom it opened up onto a quiet, protected cove area that wasn't as windy. The bleached driftwood was piled high at the edge of the bluff and the tide was out, leaving a wide swatch of white sand. I could have spent the whole afternoon there, exploring the water, the sand and the driftwood. But up on the bluff the next 200 miles of riding is waiting for me. I climbed the steep footpath back up to Jackie and the bikes, renewed by my workout.

So, on we pressed north along Highway 101 and the Pacific Ocean coast, seeing magnificent sights, one after the other, like rolling waves of endless seascape. I lost count of how many bridges we crossed over tributaries to the ocean, a vast variety of types and lengths. We also rode through the Cape Creek Tunnel along the way. The timber industry is huge in Oregon, as 47% of the land is forest. Oregon is the top producer for lumber and plywood in the country, there is evidence in every port. We saw the huge trucks bringing in the heavy logs and off-loading onto ships or at mills. At one point the equipment was turning a huge pile of wood chips that looked to be what is used for ground cover.

We reluctantly left Highway 101 and all of its splendor, just south of Newport, turned east on Highway 20 to Albany. At Albany we went north on I-5 to our hotel in Salem. This last 80 miles was all on freeway, a big adjustment from the rest of the day's ride. As we left the cool breezes of the ocean behind, the temperature rose to a comfortable 70 degrees. Our average speed was 45mph, so it took us nearly 12 hours to ride this route. Of course, this includes stops for gas, lunch, and Jackie's required daily intake of ice cream. We were surprised that Oregon has a state law that does not allow self-serving gas stations. We informed the attendant that nobody puts gas in a motorcycle but the driver. He graciously agreed and allowed us to fill our own bikes.

After nearly 400 miles, we were tired, looking forward to our warm and clean Comfort Inn. As we came down the freeway exit ramp in Salem, we were overwhelmed to see this huge homeless encampment spread all along the ramp. There were campers and trailers along the ramp and directly under the overpass, in an open but protected area, dozens of tents set up on the cement. The tents were close together with people everywhere. There were overflowing garbage cans near the edge of the street as well as a line of Port-a-Johns. As we stopped at the bottom of the ramp we were surrounded by the campers, people, tents, garbage and stench. It's like entering the city's hopelessness. After the beauty and freedom of 400 miles of glorious landscape, we are suddenly witnessing the entrapment of these unsheltered individuals, locked in this cement landscape with no place to go, but to exist, with their few possessions, where they are.

Unfortunately, our hotel was just across the freeway intersection and within easy sight of the encampment, minus some shrubbery. The presence of their sense of need was with us all night. I was somewhat uneasy about parking the bikes, but we were directed to park them next to the building in a well-lit area. Is it fair of me to worry about theft while parked here, more than any other place? How can these folks live outside here year-round with the climate crisis that we are in? How does any city handle or begin to try to help this many people? Are the homeless folks becoming just part of the landscape? Today, on Saturday, many bridges were under repair along the way. Helping the homeless people needs to take precedence as much as taking care of our infrastructure.

7-17-21 Ocean beside 101

7-17-21 Cove at Harris Beach

7-17-21 Green Hill by Ocean

7-17-21 Ocean from Path

7-17-21 Path down to Ocean

7-17-21. Bluff at Harris Beach

JULY 18, 2021
Salem, Oregon to Burlington, Washington
286 miles

Today we will be riding straight north on I-5 all the way to Burlington, Washington. This is the day that our original planned trip to Alaska, before Covid, would have brought us back from Canada into Burlington, United States. Tomorrow we will continue following the original planned route home from there.

It started out today at a cool 65 degrees with full sun, quickly rose to a pleasant mid-70s for most of the day. Eager for breakfast, we traveled just two exits north, saw food signs at Portland Rd NE, so we picked The Original Pancake House. The parking lot was full, indicating something delicious. Jackie and I were jubilant about the full, robust flavor of the coffee, our first of the day. It was served to us in a shiny green ceramic mug with the Original Pancake House raised logo in yellow. It said "Authentic Genuine Goodness". The mug felt comfortable in my hand, like it belonged there, and Jackie agreed. The cup is handmade ceramic, hand painted and fired here in Salem. We were even more jubilant that we could each buy a mug to take home with us, along with a bag of their signature coffee, specially blended, roasted and ground. To top it all off I had a unique, fluffy, light, mushroom omelet, rolled in a skillet, then oven baked, topped with a homemade mushroom sherry sauce, with strawberries on the side. Never heard of it before, I will never forget it.

Along Portland Rd. between I-5 and the Pancake House, I saw a welcoming sign that read "Grover Plumbing and Electrical Supply" in large red letters. I stopped to take a picture to text to my brothers. "Grover" is my family name, my Dad and one of my brothers were electricians. I enjoyed being reminded of my Dad, whose nickname was "Grover Monster" after the puppet on Sesame Street.

We headed north on I-5 towards Washington state. Soon after clearing Salem, there were some surprises along the way. We started seeing acres and acres of beautifully well-tended groves of trees, but did not know what the crop was. Soon enough there were multiple signs saying "Hazelnuts". I never realized that Oregon had such a massive concentration of hazelnut trees, but the state raises 99% of the hazelnuts in the United States, supporting 1300 farms statewide. The rolling, fertile landscape creates magnificent, easily recognizable vineyards as well. Each separate farm seemed to have their own unique design of support for the vines; rough-hewn wood posts holding rope in a horizontal line, while others had steel posts with the rope strung in an X. It seems that the production of wine and the farming of hazelnuts complement each other.

The I-5 is a fast moving, heavy traffic, 3 to 8 multi-lane freeway. It is ironic that freeways are considered the safest riding for motorcyclists. The flow of traffic is going one way, there are no stop signs, red lights, or pedestrians. But there is so much that we miss while riding on the freeway, mostly because of the higher speeds. We could not appreciate the smells, the atmosphere, actual experience of immersing ourselves in the hazelnut groves and the vineyards. We lose connection with the surrounding area because we have to stay focused on speed as the miles fly by under us. While crossing a bridge in Tacoma we could see a white topped mountain looming over another bridge, but we had no connection as to which mountain it was. Hopefully tomorrow's routing will allow us to actually look at the scenery and identify the mountains.

The freeway is like a world of its own. The first traffic slow-down was around Portland, then Olympia was a breeze, but in Tacoma we spent upwards of an hour going about 10 miles. We were lucky it was not hot today; the temperatures were only in the low 70's. Except for feeling trapped by the traffic, we could still enjoy the fresh air. I-5 is the main freeway and we were driving in one of 4 lanes, through the north to east curve. Then 2 lanes of Highway 16 merged in from the left, and within a mile I-5 narrowed down to 3 lanes. Then within the next mile I-705 was merging 2 more lanes in from the right. I think Tacoma has one of the most convoluted freeway systems there is. I was seeing this develop on my GPS, as well as experiencing it.

Once we got to Seattle, the largest of the four cities, we were moving at slower speeds, but steady, able to look around. The overhead speed limit signs slow the traffic by lanes as needed and kept everything rolling. Seattle was definitely the most interesting, with it's raised freeway. From that vantage point we could see at least 10 of those huge t-shaped cranes constructing high rise buildings or elevated roads. As we moved through the city there were large road projects everywhere. Talk about a city on the rise.

We got into Burlington, Washington, before 5pm to our hotel, having traveled comfortably all day. No heat exhaustion or chills to the point of needing extra layers of clothing. We were in in time for some errands, then we relaxed, had pizza in a Florida Keys style restaurant, Coconut Kenny's, decorated like an outdoor tropical hut, welcoming the atmosphere of laughter. Coming back to my bike I realize that there is nothing to laugh about. I had not washed it properly since we left Michigan. Every time I ride at home, the ritual is that my bike gets a warm soapy bath, rinsed off and dried before I back it into the garage, gleaming and happy. A moment of pride for me and my bike. We have been on the road for 18 days, I have looked almost daily for a simple, hand-held car wash and have not been able to find one yet. My bike has never been so much in need of a wash, it feels negligent to me. The shine is gone. Wiping with a cloth and spray, or using the morning dew will not do. Tonight I am in search once again for a simple, hand-held car wash, but there is none to be found.

7-18-21 Coconut Kenny's

7-18-21 Coffee Mug

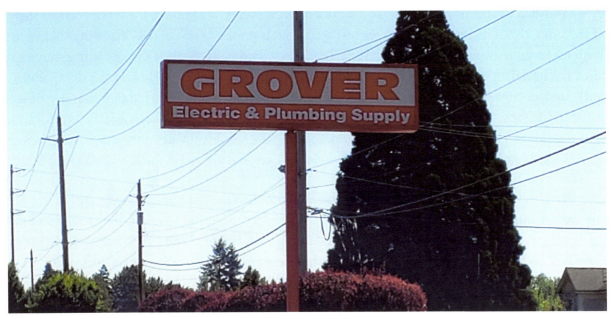

7-18-21 Grover Electric

JULY 19, 2021
Burlington, WA to Hood River, OR
316 miles

We were eager to be on secondary roads today, to experience the scenery up close. It was a cool 58 degrees as we started out. While eating breakfast we wondered about needing reservations for the ferry we planned to take from Coupeville over to Port Townsend. We phoned the ferry, learned that the next ferry out, the 10:15am was full, so we reserved 2 spots on the 11:45am trip, knowing that we were only about an hour away from the ferry. As we headed west on Hwy 29, the Olympic Range mountains formed the backdrop of our scenic view all morning, including the ferry ride and the drive along the Hood Canal, until we turn back east towards Olympia. We crossed over onto Fidalgo Island, a peaceful place of fertile farm land, with many manicured farms and fields of lush green alfalfa. We continued west and south on Hwy 29 onto Whidbey Island, through the shade of Douglas fir and western hemlock trees, rode through Oak Harbor and Coupeville to Fort Casey and arrived at the Keystone Ferry Landing.

We checked in for the 11:45am ferry ride at 10:10am. The 10:15am ferry was still at the dock! As we were signing in for the 11:45am trip that we had reservations for, the man registering us told us to go directly onto the ferry. We passed a line of waiting cars, boarded the ferry, and parked, like little people, next to a tractor trailer. It was a miracle that we were on the 10:15am ferry instead of waiting for an hour and a half for the next one. Before we could get our stuff locked up, we were under way.

The whole ferry ride was only about a half hour long, as we relaxed, surrounded by fresh air and the peace of the smooth water. Like traveling in a picture postcard, the water was a luxurious blue in contrast to the emerald green of the trees along the shoreline, and an even bluer sky. Further to the south the Olympia Range mountains break up the blues of the iridescent water and soft blue sky with their snowy white covered tops. As the ferry was approaching Port Townsend, all of the buildings seemed to welcome us in white.

Cool, fresh air with the smell of water lingered with us as we landed in Port Townsend, continued south back onto Scenic Highway 101 again. On our right were the faithful Olympia Mountains coming closer, on the left was water, first the Dabob Bay, then the Hood Canal that stretched for miles. It was 106 miles from Port Townsend to Olympia, and about 75 of those miles were along the water's edge. From the quaint little towns, to the river, to the huge forest and mountains beyond, it was a glorious ride.

Along the way, one of our stops was in Hoodsport, a small town with about two blocks of tourist shops. We wandered through beach wear, water toys, and trinkets. Big Foot standing on a corner seemed to be part of the atmosphere, along with the guy operating a distillery out of an open garage door. One shop I wandered into I saw this pottery dish with the white of the Olympia Mountain tops and the blue of the water, captured in a clam shell. I was excited to carry this little bit of heaven back home with me and add it to my collection of memories.

We rode for miles and miles with water on the left, mountains on the right, with no place to stop for a potty break. I finally spotted the Lilliwaup Store & Motel, established in 1925. The first sign inside says the bathroom is for paying customers only. Since Jackie is in need of her daily ice cream that's no problem. She asked for the bathroom and the lady crooked her finger to follow her behind the counter. A little later the lady showed me behind the counter, through a doorway into a labyrinth of boxes and paths, pointed me toward a blue door. The bathroom was about 2 feet wide and the sink was less than a foot in diameter outside the bathroom, but it was clean. There was something nostalgic and friendly about the store, right out of the 60's. The packaged ice cream was fresh, went down cool, reviving us in these mid 70's afternoon temperatures.

Once we got to Olympia, we said goodbye to the Olympia Mountain Range and 150 miles of lackadaisical scenery riding. Now we ride south on the I-5 freeway, for about 100 miles, towards Vancouver and turn east on Highway 14. Along this stretch, a new little scare happened, a first for both of us. We were running about 75 mph in the middle of 3 lanes, approaching a slower tractor trailer on our right. First, I saw small bits of something black coming toward me and got hit by some of it. Within seconds the whole retread tire came off the wheel on the left side of the trailer, in large pieces, and blew all over the highway in front of us. Fortunately, there were no vehicles close in the left lane so we were able to quickly get over and avoid most of the rubber debris. We were thankful for those couple of seconds that kept us safe.

As we came down the ramp from the I-5 freeway onto Highway 14, Jackie was shifting down, discovered her heel shift lever was gone. She could shift with just the front lever with her toe, but not easily. A few minutes later when we stopped, she found that the lever was off the shaft, but caught between the running board and the motor. A close inspection found the screw was there too. She was thinking of having to find another H-D dealership, plus cost for parts and labor. Her anger began to come down a notch. So, once we got into the hotel and the bike cooled down, she put the heel lever back on. The only damage is her nice white tennis shoe ended up with black rubber all over the toe. A couple days later the lever came loose again, but she put it back on while the motor was hot, it held this time.

Once we started east on Hwy 14, we were traveling on the north side of the Columbia River through the Gifford Pinchot National Forest, some 1.3 million acres of forest lands, water sheds and mountains, in the state of Washington. Across the river was the Mt. Hood National Forest, 1.1 million acres of forested mountains, lakes and streams in the state of Oregon. The Columbia River begins in the mountains of British Columbia, flows 1,253 miles to the Pacific Ocean, separating the states of Oregon and Washington along this stretch. This was a 2-lane curvy, hilly highway with the sun shining directly on us for the 65-mile trip to Hood River. Riding in 88-degree temperatures along the river, with forest and mountains on both sides, we were surrounded by constant panoramic views of the blue water against the green forest and the mountains. But we never felt small. It was like the panorama opened before us, like a gift of sharing with us the magic and wonder of its grandeur. The wide, cool river beside us, with its vast variety of boats and the roughness of the water kept us cool without the shade.

The top-off of the day was that I finally found a car wash and my bike got a proper, thorough cleaning.

7-19-21 Lakeshore

7-19-21. Ferry View

7-19-21. Hood canal along road

7-19-21. MT Hood National Forest across Columbia River

7-19-21. View along Hood Canal of mountains

JULY 20th, 2021
White Water Rafting on the White Salmon River
26 miles

For the past five days we have been admiring the pace and flow of the water, as we drove along the ocean, beside the rivers, across the bays. The water is inviting us to join its rhythm. Taking off our shoes and socks, standing in the Pacific Ocean was just the beginning. Today we will join the waters flow by raft along 15 miles of the White Salmon River.

We spent the night in Hood River, Oregon, on the south side of the Columbia River in a small hotel owned by a young family from India. To fortify me for this big adventure on the river, I crossed the street to the McDonalds, the lobby closed because of Covid. I walked with the cars through the drive-thru for my egg sandwich and coffee for breakfast. Jackie stuck to her coffee and food bar for her fortification. This morning we crossed back over the Columbia River, rode 13 miles up into the mountains to Husum, Washington, to the River Drifters, our host for this escapade.

We were welcomed along with 46 fellow adventurers. The excitement in the group was palpable. Wearing shorts or a bathing suit, we were fitted with farmer john style wet suits, zipper booties, a helmet, a river jacket with velcro sleeves and neck closures, to keep us warm and dry. And a life jacket and paddle, of course. Once we were suited up, we locked our purses, clothes, shoes in our bikes, turned the keys into the office color coded plastic buckets. We went empty-handed onto the rafts since nothing was allowed, including cameras.

We loaded on the bus to ride the 7 miles upriver to where the rafts awaited, but to our surprise, the bus only went 500 feet and stopped on the Husum Falls bridge. We were ushered off and shown Husum Falls from below, a notorious class 5 rapid, a 14-foot drop, the tallest floatable waterfall in the United States. Going over this rapid is commonly compared to the impact of a 35mph car crash! We were told to ponder whether we wanted to experience the waterfall in the raft, when the moment came in the ride, or be let off above and walk out to this bridge. This would be the final hurrah of the morning ride, with lunch to follow.

Jackie and I were assigned to a raft with two couples from Port Townsend, an area that we drove through yesterday. When we first started out, we were given a few instructions to get us through all of the rapids successfully, paddling together as a team. Our guide was Oscar from Costa Rico. We both realized that Oscar was going to keep us safe as we joined the movement and mood of the water. He knew every boulder, branch and turn of the river, he was part of the river. At 27 years old he had paddled all over the world. At 16 years of age, he earned a scholarship to a paddling school, as one of the top paddlers in Costa Rico. He traveled all over North and South America, completed his education of high school and 3 years of college. Oscar now works here in the United States for six months, and in Costa Rico at his own rafting guide business the other six months of the year. We relished his obvious love for the river and we trusted him to get us safely over the Husum Falls.

The whole morning was like being surrounded by shade. We have been traveling for days being able to see for miles and miles, but today we are at the bottom of a gorge, immersed with this fast-flowing river, in 42 degree splashing water, controlling our flow by paddling under safe directions from Oscar. This river is 70% fed by spring water from the surrounding mountains. The ice has melted and run down to the river within the last 12 hours. We are enjoying plenty of yellow and pink flowers and weeds along the edge, growing out of cracks in the high walls. There are also a few scrappy trees growing out of the side of the mountain with not much fortification for growth.

A couple places we had to portage around fields of huge rocks. The guides let us off at the river's edge, we left our paddles in the raft and walked or climbed along the edge for a few hundred feet to where the guides had pulled the rafts in. This portaging was not easy as we climbed over rocks, along the edge of the walls of the mountain, sloshed through weeds and mud to get to the rafts. Another time the guides let us out, then held onto ropes out to the rafts and floated them down the river unmanned. Again, we followed along the rough rivers edge, hanging onto ropes strung along the wall or metal hand holds in places, over boulders, and in the mud of the river to get back to the rafts. Immersing ourselves into the adventure of this river, first hand, on this rubber raft, was such a welcome change from riding our motorcycles mile after mile, day after day.

Then, as we approached the Husum Falls we were given detailed instructions. This is a raft that holds 6 adults maximum and the guide on the back. We had to get on the floor of the boat to go over the rapids. There is only one way to get all 6 people on the floor. We had to keep our paddle in one hand and parallel, hanging onto the outside rope that is attached all around the raft, get our feet out from under the center beam, pull our body into the fetal position on the floor, tip our head into the life jacket, and hold onto a handle on the middle cross beam with the other hand. We practiced this maneuver 6 or 7 times before the real thing. We had 5 to 6 seconds to get into this position before we went over the falls. We also got serious instructions as to what to do if we did fall out, which was to stay balled up until our head comes to the surface, then stretch our legs out in front of us, let our feet hit the rocks, float down the river until we are caught and hauled back into the boat.

The experience of leaping into space is a thrilling one, for that fraction of a second. Trusting Oscar was paramount. We were pressed tight against the raft and each other, so when we hit bottom it was a strong jolt to the whole system, like a crash. Within seconds we were untangling ourselves, getting back up on top of the raft. We cheered for ourselves, and for relief. No one fell out. Jackie sprained her thumb and one lady got an arm in the face. Oscar told us afterwards that he has yet to lose a person on this fall, but he himself has fallen out a couple of times.

Once we made it over Husum Falls we tied the raft off, climbed up the river bank, over a guard rail, onto the bridge where several spectators watched. We walked the short distance back to the River Drifters buildings. After a morning of exertion, we relished a good lunch of black beans with white rice, boneless skinless chicken roasted in basil and garlic, and watermelon.

For the afternoon ride, only 24 of the original 48 continued on. This ride was to be less big rapids and the air was warmer now, so we were allowed to take off the river jacket. This afternoon was actually a much prettier ride, with the river flowing wider, the walls not as high, less paddling with grand and glorious views. Again, we had to portage around a dangerous area, tough going for all of us. Maneuvering against the wall along rounded rocks, there was a rope strung along the rock face to hang onto, steel handholds in some places to travel over and around rocks, tall grasses and weeds. The guides didn't even ride the boats through the rapids. Instead, they tied on ropes and floated the raft through from the edge as they walked ahead of us along the same path. Once we got to the take-out location, we had to help haul the raft up a steep gravel and dirt embankment to the road edge. It took all seven of us to get it the top. Everyone taller than me (I'm 5'2") lifted the raft up onto a high carry rack that was pulled behind the bus.

As we returned to the hotel, Jackie and I talked about our adventure on the White Salmon River, and felt a sense of gratitude. As our ride on the river was coming to a conclusion with the river widening out into shallows before flowing into the Columbia River, there was an "a-ha" moment. That's when we startled a Great Blue Heron that flew over us, showing off his impressive size and shagginess, while a deer was drinking in the shallows, at peace with our appearance and laughter. In the distance we could see snow-capped Mt. Hood, at an 11,250 feet elevation, in all of its splendor, the only spot open for skiing this week in the world.

We had a sense of contentment with our day on the river. It had worn us out. While I was taking a shower Jackie ordered our pizza. When the pizza was delivered there were also two boxes of Chocolate Lava Crunch Cakes, two in a box, warm, from Dominoes. It was warm, crunchy on the outside, chocolate cake with liquid dark chocolate inside. An explosion of chocolate to end the day.

7-20-21 Mt Hood

7-20-21 Rafting

7-20-21. River Drifters at Husum, Wa.

7-20-21. White Salmon River edge

JULY 21, 2021
Hood River, Oregon to Twin Falls, Idaho
500 miles

Today was a whirl wind kind of day. Yesterday the bikes sat and rested while we were immersed in the closeness of the water and river gorge walls, with flowers, weeds and mud. Today we have to complete 500 miles speeding across the open prairies. Again, I started the day fortified with egg McMuffins from McDonalds across the street. I walked in line with the cars through the drive-thru. We left Hood River about 7:40am in a cloudy 63 degrees, dressed warmly in light sweatshirt, riding jacket and gloves.

We headed southeast on I-84, traveling along the south side of the Columbia River. Near the town of Boardman was a gigantic coal fired power plant with electric lines and poles seriously marring the scenery. The plant was shuttered in 2020 and the building will be demolished in 2022. The power collection has been replaced with solar panels and windmills to end decades of air pollution.

Then we moved away from the Columbia River, into the high desert country with its yellows, browns and golds across the miles, like a Van Gogh painting. We rode through the land of the Umatilla Indian Reservation, watched the brown tumbleweed bouncing and rolling in the wind. There was something wistful like the wild west movies, with the tumbleweed tumbling over and over, as we sped along with the miles rolling under us.

As we came around a sweeping curve, the Pendleton View Point appeared high up on top of a butte, enticing us to take a quick rest, although there was no shade to be found. The landscape of yellow grass spread out for miles and miles below us, but only a single farm could be seen. As we continued southeast for 200 miles, the desolate terrain changed into butte formations, then back to high desert, with mountains off to the northeast. The landscape was like a pitch and rhythm to our speed and the music in our ears. There was no human life to be seen, no herds of cattle. No farms, no ranches, no people seen camping, or playing on quad runners, or even horses. Just the tumbleweeds to keep us company.

We went over the Snake River and crossed into Idaho. Solar windmills appeared across the tops of rock. A narrow strip of solar panels, about 30 feet wide, stretched for several miles along the freeway beside us. Dairy farms and beef cattle began to appear along the way. A lot of farms were watering the crops and I could smell wet corn stalks. The pastures were also being watered, the cattle stood there steaming, soaking it up.

We cruised all day, mile after mile, hour after hour at a steady speed of 75mph, as the landscape melted around us. My secret sustenance for the day was my one remaining decadent chocolate lava cake that I saved from last night. I nibbled on it at each break along the way as we rode 500 miles in just over nine hours. The temperatures rose all day and were now in the high 90's as we crossed the southern portion of Idaho. Most of the day there was cloud cover that gave us the needed shade to travel this far in this heat. We sailed into Twin Falls under a little bit of rain. Crossing the Perrine Memorial Bridge over the Snake River, we saw signage for the Shoshone Water Falls, welcoming us to further explorations tomorrow.

7-21-21 Indian Reservation

7-21-21. Farm from Pendleton View Point

7-21-21. Umatilla Indian Reservation

JULY 22, 2021
Twin Falls, Idaho to West Yellowstone, Montana
286 miles

Today we found something we had not expected. It was not on our plans that we had so carefully mapped out. We had noted most of the scenic attractions coming our way but had missed this one. It was like a gift.

There was some small signage directing us to the park, as we descended down a narrow, switch-back road to an outcropping of rock, surrounded by a pristine park, to view the falls. At 3,255 feet elevation, Shoshone Falls plummets over rocky, horseshoe shaped canyons carved by the Snake River, falling 212 feet. It is 900 feet wide, one of the largest natural water falls in the United States, surpassing the height of the famous Niagara Falls. Shoshone Falls was like a gift of pleasure; the sight, the sound and the spray were all encompassing and I was in awe. Absolutely gorgeous and spectacular could not describe this find. When a rainbow appeared in the spray of the falls, with its riot of colors – red, orange, yellow, green, blue, indigo and violet - in the water droplets, we felt the shelter and hope paving our way through the miles we have come and the miles we will go.

I have fond memories of the Snake River. In the early 80's I went on a week-long rafting trip, starting and ending in Idaho, looping through both Washington and Oregon states. The river was wide, open in places, or coiled through bottoms of deep gorges, but no large waterfalls as here in southern Idaho. The Snake River begins in the mountains of Wyoming, works its way through Idaho, Oregon and Washington, like a snake, before dumping into the Columbia River, having traveled some 1,078 miles. Yesterday we crossed the Snake River twice, once at the border of Oregon and Idaho and to get into Twin Falls on our drive here.

We realized that we have to leave the beauty of the falls and start our travel day. We stopped at the local Snake Harley-Davidson dealership because Jackie wanted her clutch adjusted, but learned that it is hydraulic so she has to live with it. We toured the clothing area and Jackie was excited to find a coat that she had wanted for two years.

Finally, about 11:20am we hit the freeway, riding east out of Twin Falls at an elevation of 3200 feet on I-84 and then northeast on I-86, generally following along the path of the Snake River. At Chubbuck we turned north on I-15, away from the river, rode through the Fort Hall Indian Reservation, into Idaho Falls. Idaho is a checkerboard of land forms. From high desert, to farm fields, to river beds, to cattle country, to mountains; it was a constantly changing view all day. But what stayed constant was the mountains in the distance, they kept getting closer as we rose in elevation. At some point I realized that I could see mountains over one shoulder as far as I could see, and all the way around over the other shoulder, 270 degrees. One of the beauties of riding a 3-wheel motorcycle.

At Idaho Falls we turned off onto Highway 20, a divided highway up to Sugar City. North of Sugar City the road turned to two lanes for the rest of the ride into West Yellowstone, at an elevation of 6,667 feet. About 40 miles outside of West Yellowstone, Highway 20 crossed into Montana, with the state line dividing the Caribou & Custer Gallatin National Forests. The Custer Gallatin National Forest, some 3.1 million acres, is one of the largest wilderness areas in the United States, encompassing the Greater Yellowstone Echo System. After we crossed over a small mountainous range, the land became flat and fertile. The further north we rode the landscape turned lush green, until we drove for miles and miles through this sensational forest of Douglas fir, spruce, white fir, lodgepole and mountain hemlock pine trees.

We arrived at our hotel, the Days Inn Wyndham in West Yellowstone, at a comfortable 83 degrees. We started the day with jackets on at 63 degrees, temperatures rising through the day to as high as 89, with 10 minutes of cooling rain late in the day. For dinner we were directed to The Branch, a restaurant inside the Holiday Inn. Outside of the building, between the street and sidewalk, was a set of train tracks, highlighted by the vibrant colors of red and yellow summer flowers in two barrels. Inside the building was a full-sized sleeper train car, the Oregon Short Line rail car, on display on the track. This railroad car was decommissioned in 1935 and used as a cottage for multiple owners until 1995. It was then restored to museum quality, placed on the tracks, with the Holiday Inn built around it. Touring this railway car, reading the descriptions on the back of the menu and talking about it as we waited for our order; then savoring a fancified meal, made for a satisfying evening.

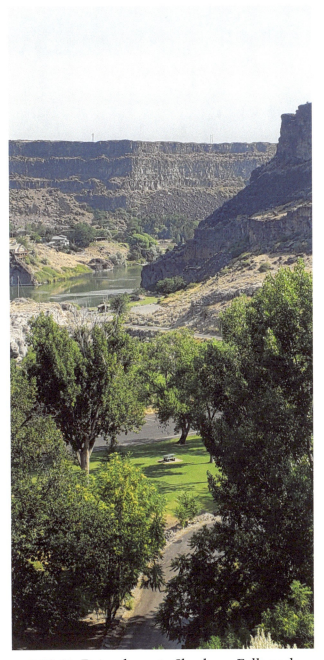

7-22-21. Drive down to Shoshone Falls park

7-22-21. Shoshone Falls

7-22-21. Us at Shoshone Falls

7-22-21.Oregon Short Line rail car

JULY 23, 2021
West Yellowstone, Montana to Cody, Wyoming
150 miles

We started out the day at a cool 67 degrees, eager to visit Yellowstone National Park. First, we had to ship another box of our treasurers back home. While we were at Pack Mail, I talked to a guy from Texas, about 50 years old, who was also shipping stuff back home. He was riding from the border of Mexico to the border of Canada on the Continental Divide, the off-road route, on a large dirt- style motorcycle. At this point he was nursing a knee injury, worrying if he could finish the trip. He was using a GPS and the trail was marked, but he said he had gotten lost a couple of times. We had crossed the divide back in New Mexico, so I was shocked at how far he had come, the terrain of mountains, high plains, forest, and buttes that he must have crossed. I understood what an unbelievable undertaking this would be.

This was the first time for me to visit Yellowstone National Park. We joined other tourists in the heavy traffic, in a stop and go pattern for about 20 miles because of wildlife. There he was, the American bison, this big, gnarly, mangy animal peacefully munching the grass along beside the road. I could smell him, he was that close. King of his domain, completely ignoring the business around him, the people taking pictures safely from inside their cars and their excitement of his presence. On our motorcycles we were a little nervous, having no protection from this overgrown fellow. Moving with caution, we were glad our bikes are quiet, not roaring, to disturb him from his grazing.

I was so awed with the presence and majesty of the bison that I took him home with me as a memory in a small ceramic vase found at the gift store. He is just as shaggy and fearsome, charging to attack, in a black silhouette with pine trees, the mountains in the distance, and an eagle, on a slate gray background.

The road through the park from the west traveled along beside a peaceful, picturesque river for several miles. It was like paradise with a backdrop of tall green lodgepole pines and the mountains. Riding along the river's edge we could hear the water burbling, chuckling over the rocks. It was pretty in the morning sunlight. Our first stop was at a field of hot springs at Firehole Lake. We had to wait for a parking spot. Boardwalks have been built out and along through the fields of hot springs. We were warned not to go off from the boardwalk because of the heat and immanent death. We took the circular boardwalk out among the bubbling, steamy, toxic smelling, vegetation killing springs coming out of the ground. The hot water was running out onto the ground making mud, colored with mineral run-off. Without a doubt, the landscape in Yellowstone National Park is breathtaking. When taking a breath at Firehole Lake there is something in the air that smells like rotten eggs, like sulfuric acid, which was unpleasant but memorable.

We worked our way through the park, constantly climbing upward, until we got to Old Faithful, at 7,350 feet elevation. At Old Faithful the incredible amount of people was phenomenal. We were blown away with it. The parking lot was huge and full, people were 4 deep all the way around the geyser. Where did all of these people come from? The geyser erupts about 20 times a day, up to four minutes each time with approximately 2000 people present for every eruption. Securing a seat at Old Faithful can be challenging. Folks can actually download an app on their phone that will give them the time of the next eruption. We could not get close enough to even see the surrounding area, but it had to be much like Firehole Lake. From a distance we saw Old Faithful, stealing the show with her billowy plums of pressurized steam shooting high into the air. Carefully threading our way through the cars and people, we made our exit before folks made the mad dash back to their cars. I realized just how big this park is when we traveled through the rest of the park all day, and didn't see many people.

The Park is stunningly beautiful. Sitting in the heart of Yellowstone Park is Yellowstone Lake, that runs 20 miles x 14 miles across and sits at an elevation of 7,744 feet. It is the largest fresh water lake, above 7,000 feet elevation, in North America. Yellowstone Lake freezes completely over in the winter and has an average temperature of 41 degrees. We rode about 50 miles of the 110 miles of shoreline, traveling north, then east along the west and north shores. The air was hazy over the lake, muting our view of the splendor of pine trees and snow-capped mountains in the distance.

Once we crossed the bridge at the north end of Yellowstone Lake,

our scenery turned deadly, changing from unending splendor of verdant green forests pulsing with life, to this complete black devastation in the blink of an eye. For miles and miles along East Entrance Road we rode on, shocked and saddened, through the landscape of burned sticks, the remainder of trees standing like skeletons in an eerie salute to the fires that ripped the area apart. On the burned, blackened ground lonely logs lay withering and bleaching in the sun. To see this destruction was beyond my comprehension.

It was the bright purplish-red, reddish-purple clusters of flowers shyly appearing along the gray dead log that renewed our spirits. This gave us hope and a sign of renewal. Fireweed is a tall, showy wildflower that rapidly colonizes areas burned by fire. We wanted to believe that soon this blackened, devastated area of meadows, forests, streams and road edges would be carpeted with bright magenta flowers, like laughter.

We kept climbing, headed for the east gate and topped out at 8,530 feet elevation along Sylvan Pass, located in the Absaroka Range. Sylvan Pass is an approximate 77 mile stretch of highway that includes East Entrance Road and North Fork Hwy, from Lake Village in Yellowstone National Park to Cody, Wyoming. This road was a two-lane narrow blacktop snaking through the mountains on a steep, curvy path that at times was scary. From high mountain walls beside us, to deep valleys below us, with no guardrails to protect us from oblivion. The pine forests were thick and deeply green, such a contrast to the black devastation we had just come through. We stopped once near the top, just along beside the road to get a view of a deep valley below. The height of the mountain has come into my legs, they are like rubber as I look down to the valley below. Am I feeling the lack of oxygen up here?

After hitting the heights of Sylvan Pass, it was a relief to start the five-mile descent downward, controlling our speed through a jumble of trees and rocks in quick succession on both sides with the North Fork Shoshone River paralleling along beside us. We came down out of the mountains to a jubilant view of a valley of vast horse ranches and cowboys that roamed along with the river all the way to the Buffalo Bill Reservoir, on into Cody, Wyoming. This 52-mile stretch of the North Fork Shoshone River highway between the east entrance of Yellowstone National Park to Cody, was called "the most scenic 52 miles in America" by Teddy Roosevelt.

As we continued riding on the North Fork Hwy along the North Fork Shoshone River, it was slowly getting wider. The water from the river was muddy brown as it fed down out of the mountains, until it joined the deep blue waters of the Buffalo Bill Reservoir. To see the brown and blue waters blending together captivated us as we rode along above the rim of this huge lake. The mountains were solid rock on our left, close to us. There was a rock wall across the water that seemed to be coming closer.

Then we rounded a bend to see a solid wall of rock coming together in a V with the lake a very deep blue. Parking was immediate so we stopped for a break. When we continued, within 500 feet further around the bend, that we could not see when parked, was the surprise of the Buffalo Bill Dam, at 325 feet. It is named after the famous William "Buffalo Bill" Cody, who founded the nearby town of Cody and owned much of the land. Surprisingly, next to the Dam, the road continued through a quarter mile long tunnel, through two more shorter tunnels and over a large bridge, before we were again driving among the horse ranches.

Shortly thereafter we arrived in Cody at our hotel, the Kings Inn, at 91 degrees. To add to our surprises, there was a kingdom of taxidermy mounted animals from Africa in the lobby! The staff said that the hotel next door was owned by the same man, full of animals taken in North America. The owner of both hotels had shot all of these animals and had them mounted. We were welcome to go over and take a look, but I was not impressed. I did not go next door. The owner had made an African theme hotel, offering free breakfasts, an indoor pool, and stuffed animals, but he had no elevator to the upper floors. So, for the benefit of the well-being of the animals, we had to hire a young fellow to carry our heaviest bags up the stairs for us.

Now, you would think that we had enough adventures for today: Yellowstone National Park geysers, Old Faithful, a bison, the Yellowstone Lake, the burned forest, the Absaroka mountains, the North Fork Shoshone River and the Buffalo Bill Reservoir and Dam. You would think that our sense of wonder and awe would be complete, after all that. But there was one more pinnacle to reach.

Cody is the Rodeo Capital of the World, since 1938, longest running and only nightly rodeo, June to August, in the world. So off we went to the Rodeo, in the cool of the evening, just a mile down the road, for two hours of wild western action and music, laughing and enjoying the show with the other tourists and the friendly folks from town. There were cattle roping, bronco horse-back riding, barrel racing, and the flag show.

For me, the final celebration of our very full day was the lady doing trick riding with her horse. It began with her standing up on the saddle, with the horse at a gentle walk, carrying the American Flag in full array on a tall pole. But as the opening ceremony went on, the horse kept increasing in speed as it circled the arena at least 10 times, until they were at a full out gallop. With her still standing on top of the saddle, with wild west dexterity, waving the American Flag on its pole as high as she could reach.

7-23-21 Mountain in Yellowstone

7-23-21 Buffalo Bill Reservoir

7-23-21 Yellowstone Bison

7-23-21 Yellowstone burn w flowers

7-23-21 Yellowstone geysers

7-23-21 Yellowstone river

7-23-21. Geyser field

JULY 24, 2021
Cody, Wyoming to Spearfish, South Dakota
345 miles

Cody is a cowboy town with a cowboy flavor: lots of ranches, horses and cattle. We relished its western hospitality from the Rodeo last night to breakfast this morning at The Station by Cody Coffee, originally a gas station. French roasted artisan coffee and breakfast sandwiches, in their modern vibe Wyoming style outdoor seating, complete with a fire pit, inspired us for our ride up through the mountains to Spearfish, South Dakota.

We left Cody at about 73 degrees, headed northeast on Alternate 14, all the way to I-90 at Ranchester, about 140 miles. This was a 2-lane paved road with little to no shoulder, a speed limit of 70mph. For the first 75 miles or so we enjoyed the views of large ranches spread out before us, quiet, dry, dusty. Cattle and horses roamed the pastures. The small towns were home style and comfortably old fashioned.

We were riding on a raised roadway; below us was a large, flat area of mud with green and dark brown grasses, normally seen underwater. The GPS had us crossing a large lake, except there was no water around us. The lake had dried up. After about a mile we crossed a 50-foot-wide river, all that was left of the lake. This was a picture of global warming at its worst.

The further east we rode, climbing steadily upward in the mountains, the land became more desolate, and rocky, less tillable. Population disappeared, so did the horses and the cows and the towns. Miles upon miles of prairie pockmarked with stubbles of weeds and stones, like we are riding through a western movie set with crevices, valleys, walls, hills, to hide and seek. We are in the Bighorn National Forest, a mixture of grasslands, sheer mountain walls, crystal clear lakes and teeming rivers. The Bighorn Mountains are a sister range of the Rocky Mountains that are situated halfway between Yellowstone National Park and Mt. Rushmore.

All this time we are climbing higher and higher in the mountains. We entered the Medicine Wheel Passage, 27 miles of scenic by-way, at an elevation of 9,642 feet. The air has turned to a cool 67 degrees and getting thinner, more difficult to breathe. We came around a curve to a sign that said "Steep Grades Next 20 Miles". In the next 20 miles it was like riding a bronco, going up, going

around, going down a little then right back up and up, riding through steep canyon terrain, all around curves, all along the side of a mountain, then more uphill and more curves. My hands on the handlebars were frequently as high as my shoulders to match the high gradient of the road. True switchback roads that were rough from patching, four inches of blacktop in a two-inch hole, for several feet, several times. So, add that to the bronco ride. We were now at about 12,000 feet above sea level, the highest point that I have ever been in the United States.

We finally stopped at a wide spot on the side of the mountain, desolate with small shrubs in gravel. I avoided looking down over the edge when we were coming up the mountain. The heights were dizzying. Looking down and seeing green forest below, the spikes of trees, and the valleys laid out before us gave me a sense of total accomplishment and celebration, that we have come this far, to this height in America.

The drive down was steep and curvy, narrow with deep cliffs dropping away beside us. The dense forest reappeared, surrounding us. With the trees closing us in, keeping an eye on the GPS gave me reassuring warning of the coming curves. After about 5 miles steeply downhill, we relaxed as the road leveled off. Then suddenly another 10 miles of downward, steep grade, out onto the high plains heading to Ranchester. A herd of wild horses roamed the plains, grazing freely in the distance, giving us a sense of home coming.

Cattle ranches began to show up along the way. At two separate locations vacationers were camping off the beaten path in the high plains, gathered to enjoy the area with their modern trucks and expensive trailers or motorhomes. Along the way we saw locals with their big trucks and quad-runners gathered to ride or hunt. At another point, just off the side of the road, there were 4 vehicles and several native Americans filling containers from a free-flowing water spout out of the mountain side.

We left behind our precarious adventures in the mountains, continuing across the high plains on I-90/I-14, 200 miles of freeway, in 94-degree heat, wide-open and fast, all the way to Spearfish, South Dakota. The speed limit was 80mph for cars, trucks and semis. We were running our usual 75mph but the tractor trailers would bear down on us, fly by, and just disappear. We sped up to 85mph at times to keep from getting run over, but they still passed us by. This was disconcerting, like being attacked, because we are so small compared to these tractor trailers. Such a hair on fire experience after the preferred peace and loneliness of climbing the Big Horn Basin. The heat added to the trauma of the afternoon as we sped across these high plains. No shade to be found anywhere.

After this mad rush on the freeway, we were glad to arrive safely for the next three days, at the home of Chris, a friend of Jackie's. The house is perched on the side of a mountain, surrounded by shade, at about 3600 feet elevation. A flock of wild turkeys greeted us in the back yard as well as several deer coming in to feed. We felt comfortable in his large, air-conditioned home with orchids in the windowsills.

7-24-21 Desolation of Big Horn Mountains

7-24-21 Forest below us along 14A

7-24-21 Peaceful along 14A

7-24-21 Ranch Country 14A Wyoming

7-24-21 Road behind us in Big Horn Mountains

7-24-21. Nancy in the Big Horn Mountains

JULY 25, 2021
Needles State Park & Mt. Rushmore
226 miles

With the flock of wild turkeys grazing in the background, I ate a relaxing home-cooked breakfast on the screened porch at Chris' house. We left around 9:30am, in perfect weather of about 78 degrees, heading for Needles State Park and Mt. Rushmore.

We took the I-90 freeway initially for about 11 miles down to the Deadwood exit, where we connected with Highway 385. We meandered through several comfortable small towns jammed with people, vehicles everywhere, not a square of sidewalk to walk on. Crossing a bridge over Pactola Reservoir, we enjoyed lots of boats playing on the water, the coolness of the 150-foot-deep lake radiating around us. We continued all the way down this 2-lane, no shoulder road, in the valley of the mountains of the Black Hills National Forest, amidst residential homes and small farms. After deciding that we missed the turn-off into Needles, I put the location into the GPS. Following the route given we discovered this time the GPS was wrong, it had us turning left into the J-Bar Ranch, rather than right onto the road to Needles County Park. This was a reminder for me that a working knowledge of the area we are traveling is necessary, rather than to trust the GPS. It could get us into all kinds of trouble.

Entering Needles was a second trip for both of us, but it was still like traveling a scavenger hunt, feeling lost as we ride among rugged canyons, gulches, deep green forests, camping parks, meadows with birch and aspen trees, mountains, riding on narrow, winding roads, at a safe speed of about 25mph. It's up and down and all around for 50 miles, not knowing where you are, just immersed in its strange beauty. We drove through mostly forest with outcroppings of eroded granite pillars, towers and spires, including five narrow tunnels. The red and white spires of the Cedar Mesa Sandstone give Needles its name. Mountains enveloped us with drop-offs at the cliff edges, causing us to be carefully apprehensive. At one point, we came down around one of the many hairpin curves, out of the forest to a welcome surprise. There was a herd of buffalo just at the edge of the road, in a large meadow, oblivious to the large traffic jam they were causing. The herd of 60 to 75 buffalo were quietly grazing in the sun.

The Black Hills National Forest encompasses 1.2 million acres in the area. Needles is a part of that, involving Needles County Park, State Park and National Park. Riding through all of these parks, with their many turn-offs and private areas, constant turns gave us a sense of not knowing where we were. Lost but happy, we accomplished the scavenger hunt of Needles and arrived at Mt. Rushmore with the temperatures now in the low 90's. Thankfully we parked in the covered parking garage, the coolness of the cement and the shade were welcome.

Imagine, arriving at the splendor of Mt. Rushmore with its majestic stone carvings of the four key presidents, and not be awe inspired. But we were so totally focused on the ice cream shop just inside the gate, before the awe hit us. We stood in the shade eating ice cream in this excessive heat, wondering how a monument exuding such a sense of freedom and democracy in the past, has now become for some, the height of white supremacy. The Avenue of Flags, 56 proud flags represent 50 states, 1 district, 3 territories and 2 Commonwealths, were waving their various colors in the breeze below the monument. These were added as part of the Bicentennial Celebration of the United States in 1976. It's hard to believe that 45 years later this symbol of unity is struggling to remain United.

The afternoon temperatures continued to rise, and topped out at 96 degrees. We left Mt. Rushmore, drove straight to the freeway, returned to Spearfish on I-90, running into a little rain on the way. We were instructed to be back to Chris's house by 4pm to go to dinner.

Once back we changed into shorts for our dinner adventures, got into his 4-wheel drive Ranger for a ride up the mountain. The food cooler is strapped in on the backseat next to me, Jackie was in the front. The cooler being strapped in should have told me something, should have been my signal, but I missed it. Through town on paved roads for about 5 miles, then a couple miles of gravel, seemed normal. Then we left the road and all hell broke loose; trees, rocks and drop-offs, logs and mud holes and bigger rocks and trenches, sand and running deer, the rest of the way up the mountain. You name it, we went over, around or through it. Sometimes on a trail and sometimes not. Chris was so familiar with the rhythm and pace of the trail, he knew where we were going, nothing marked. I now understand a little, the hair-raising experience of off-road buggy riding. I was thankful to be securely buckled in as we cruised up the side of the mountain, but seriously wondered if I should have had a helmet on. I wondered how the food in the cooler was doing. Jackie in the front seat was hanging on for dear life, watching the forest floor fall away beside her. It took a full hour to climb 2000 feet elevation to get to Chris's cottage, built on the side of the mountain, at Spearfish Canyon Rim.

His cottage hangs out over the edge of a cliff. Standing on the porch you can reach out and touch the tops of tall lodgepole pines from below. We can see for miles out over the trees, or down into the forest and valley below. Chris built this cottage himself and it sleeps 9, two in the main bedroom, 7 in the loft. There was no electricity or running water, although there was a generator. He brought up everything we needed in that cooler for dinner, except the grill, which was locked in a storage room off the porch. While I roamed around the nearby terrain, Jackie stayed safely on the porch behind the railing.

Chris grilled steaks for dinner, along with potato and macaroni salads. After our harrowing ride up the mountain, we were hungry. As we sat outside on the porch, in the top of the trees, enjoying dinner together in the peace and silence, we were struck by the isolation of this place. Nothing but the sound of the trees moving in the wind. Kind as Chris was, a perfect host, he even served us carrot cake for dessert.

We took a leisurely, shorter route back down the mountain, the forest friendly and accommodating, giving us their face instead of flying by in a rush.

We arrived back at the main house just before dark, thankful for a full day of experiencing the heartbeat of the Black Hills Mountains.

7-25-21 Cabin in the Mountains

7-25-21 Mt. Rushmore from Needles Park

7-25-21 Nancy at Mt. Rushmore

7-25-21. Jackie at Mt. Rushmore

7-25-21. Mt. Rushmore

7-25-21. Needles

7-25-21. The view from the cottage.

JULY 26, 2021
Shopping in Sturgis, South Dakota
40 miles

Today was promising to be an unusually hot day, 100 degrees by later afternoon. We spent the early morning enjoying the cool of the shade, having coffee, seated at this large table outside, with nature surrounding us. The wild turkeys and deer in the yard, peacefully grazing close by. Chris had collected the antler sheds of deer, weaving them together into a U-shaped wire trellis at the end of the table. A creative architecture, the white honeycomb of bone supporting climbing ivy. Like the orchid in the window sill, wild with flowers, and the garden filled with vegetables, Chris's place had a sense of friendliness and fun.

By around 10am we decided to brave the heat and ride to Sturgis. It was already 85 degrees. We cancelled our planned trip to the Badlands because of the heat. The bikes were ready to go, to be displayed in Sturgis, having been cleaned last night after the rain. Sturgis is motorcycle heaven with 500K bikes descending on it from August 6 to 15th, hosted by the local Harley-Davidson store. The Sturgis rally is one of the oldest in the world, including 10 days and nights of riding exhibitions, racing, shows, music, food and vendors. The very first motorcycle rally held here was in 1938, having missed a couple years, this is the 81st anniversary. Wanting to avoid the crowds, we planned to arrive now, two weeks, early to enjoy the vendors which were open and advertising their wares.

There was a swelter of vendors in the heat spread out in air-conditioned buildings for three blocks on each side, with bars on every corner. The store fronts are only open one month a year. During the rally they leave their doors and windows open for the air-conditioning to spill out onto the street, with a friendly, welcoming atmosphere. The streets were not yet blocked off, so we parked on display on the main street, proud of our bikes. We wandered in and out of every store, filled and overflowing, ready for the crowds to arrive next week. We were able to leisurely browse in every store and have fun because the crowds were sparse. There were t-shirts, sweatshirts, jackets, hats, belts, jeans, boots, jewelry, gloves, motorcycle parts, leather everything, banners, signs and flags. Harley- Davidson was the star of the show, with Jackie finding many treasures. I found the perfect purple police hat, with two mirror headlights. If I had worn it while on road patrol years ago, I would have been the star. The laughter would have taken the sting out of the tickets, accidents, thefts and fights of the day. When Jackie told me not to let her buy anything more, we knew it was time to go.

By the time we left Sturgis about 2:30pm, it was 98 degrees and climbing. Our motorcycles were standing proud in full display, baking in the sun on Main Street. To get back to Chris's house we had to ride 20 gruesome miles in the stifling heat. It was like an oven experience. Traveling at 75mph on the freeway, it was like baking something in the oven, you open the door a little, that blast of heat in your face, but constant. I am thankful for the liquid cooled engine so the heat from the motor was limited. Add the wind and the sun and a few clouds, we were overjoyed to get back to the shade and the comfort of Chris's place.

As we sat leisurely eating our last meal with Chris, a flock of wild turkeys wandered happily around the back yard, along with three doe and two bucks. It felt like home. Tomorrow we are leaving to continue our journey into the unknown, having already come 6300 miles so far, over 26 days. We spent the evening getting organized, doing laundry, packing our bags, getting ready to say goodbye to shade and comfort. We have a long, hot 485-mile ride up to Devil's Lake in northeast North Dakota tomorrow. The temperatures are going to be 100+ degrees while we travel. We are planning to leave by 6am to beat the heat. We don't need any more days where the wallet ends up in the cooler.

7-26-21 Deer at Chris's

7-26-21 Nancy in hat in Sturgis

7-26-21. Orchid in the windowsill.

7-26-21. Trellis made from antler sheds

JULY 27, 2021
Spearfish, South Dakota to Devils Lake, North Dakota
485 miles

After the kindness, hospitality and enjoyment of Chris's house for three days, we were fully rested to conquer the next 485 miles. The temperatures were expected to hit 104 degrees in Bismarck, North Dakota this afternoon on our route, so we left Chris's house at 6:20am at a cool and comfortable 61 degrees.

We headed north on Highway 85, eager to discover new territory, straight up to Belfield, North Dakota. North of Spearfish, the terrain turned into rolling desolate grazing land. We are now entering cow country. There were hundreds of cows on the prairie, brown and black dots spread out across the landscape. Then we rode for several miles across desolate land, before once again, the brown and black dots would spread across the prairie. In between the herds of cattle, we saw several antelope, only one or two together, never more. One big buck with his velvet antlers proudly stood between the roadway and the fenced pastures, watching us as we sped by. All of the bucks that we have seen in the last few days were dressed in velvet, one with a large rack.

After two hours of cows and prairie we were ready for breakfast at Buffalo, South Dakota. The No. 3 Café & Bar was the only restaurant in town. It was a friendly place, three people playing cards. Even the bathroom was friendly, two toilets and no partition between the two. Breakfast was friendly too. I had the casserole with eggs on top of Café potatoes tossed with smoked ham, sausage, tomato, onion, cheddar and Monterey jack cheese with hollandaise sauce and morning bread. Jackie was happy with cinnamon scented steel cut oats, pecans and brown sugar.

After such a feast, we were eager for new landscape. The cows disappeared and rock took over as we neared Ludlow in South Dakota. The further north we went, more rock appeared among the sparse grasses. Near the north edge of South Dakota there was nothing, no cattle, no ranches, no fields. For miles and miles just lonely, rocky, flat prairie for 50 miles. Shortly after entering North Dakota, the terrain changed once again, and crops appeared. The wheat fields were already harvested, stubble standing bleached in the sun. The corn looked pale and short for late July, due to drought. Where the blue of rivers should etch the landscape there was only dry, dusty riverbed, or just a trickle of water.

Once we got up near Belfield, North Dakota, we started seeing oil wells, like cranes bobbing up and down, hiccupping the landscape. We passed a 150-acre, state-of-the-art crude oil refinery, under construction by Davis Refinery. It is being built in close proximity to the two main highways, Highway 85 running north and south, I-94 running east and west, as well as an east, west train track with oil and gas pipelines. It is expected to be up and running by 2023, giving the area a boost in employment.

We are now leaving low traffic riding on a two lane, no shoulder Highway 85 at 70mph cruising speed, to enter eastbound I-94, a freeway with heavy truck traffic and a cruising speed of 75mph. Having enjoyed the lack of traffic on Highway 85, we now have to be more alert, more concentrated to make the quick change of riding among the speeding tractor-trailers. The terrain continued to vary from pastures to crop fields. Most of the wheat has just been harvested, the straw baled or in the process, with five or six combines or balers, in an offset line, clearing the fields like grasshoppers. In order to use every acre, the grass between the roadway and the fence or field line, 75 to 100 feet, is also being harvested Along I-94 there was a tractor and baler keeping pace with the traffic. In both North and South Dakota, they cut and bale that grass, about three strips wide.

As we were approaching New Salem, North Dakota, the highlight of our surprise for the day gradually appeared, like a speck in the distance. Over five miles we watched it grow, the closer we got the bigger it became. We laughed to see the world's largest Holstein cow, Salem Sue, overlooking the interstate on the only hill visible for several miles, New Salem's pride and joy. Measuring in at 38 feet tall and 50 feet wide, she is six tons of reinforced fiberglass, so big she was built in three sections to get her up the hill. New Salem is cow crazy, its high school sports teams are named the Holsteins. The New Salem Lions Club had her built in honor of the local farming industry in 1974.

We continued east to Steele, where we exited I-94 and took to the side roads, Highway 3N. We meandered our way, the first 41 miles on unlined pavement with no shoulder, north and east towards Devil's Lake. This was an area of small family farms set close to the road, in amongst the many small lakes that peppered the whole route. We laughed when we passed the many brilliant yellow sunflower fields gracing the countryside. North Dakota is considered one of the happiest states in the United States, producing 40% of the sunflower crop nationwide. Sunflowers reach up to the sun, its namesake. Today they were drooping because of the heavy cloud cover prevailing overhead. We appreciated the clouds and lower temperatures on our ride, but the sun flowers were sad.

Continuing north on Highway 3N the sunflower fields disappeared, giving way to mostly lakes and weedy fields. We still have about 100 miles to ride, before we arrive at our destination in Devils Lake. We pulled off the road in the middle of nowhere, onto a field driveway for a drug stop. Jackie is suffering from a head cold that needed medicating. I needed a dose of Tylenol for new little road worthy aches and pains that I didn't have a month ago.

Now that we have medicated ourselves on Tylenol, we are good to go. The bikes however needed a pit stop too, for gas. We weren't worried, my mapping directed us to continue for a few miles, turn right onto Highway 200, a well-traveled road with towns where we can get gas. However, when we got to the point that my GPS indicated, it was a field path to nowhere. We were getting concerned, nothing like watching the orange needle go down toward empty. We drove another mile further, were relieved to find Highway 200. Now we just have to find those two towns. We were getting fairly low on gas. Jackie was worrying about having AAA bring us some. The relief of the first town turned to dismay. It did not have a gas station; it didn't even have paved streets. The next town also didn't have a gas station or paved streets. Another 20 miles of anxiousness, making ourselves as light as possible, we came into the town of Carrington. It was like a gold mine, after 50 miles of worrying, with about 10 miles left on the tanks, there was a gas station. Our bikes were no doubt relieved.

In the relief and joy of getting gas, we were looking for a celebration. A lady at the gas station recommended The Ice Cream Shoppe, just ½ mile north. It was one sweet little ice cream shop. Our reward for the 50 miles of anxiety was a double chocolate peanut butter ice cream for Jackie and an orange yogurt for me. The whole thing turned into a bit of a party. Our servers had fun dishing up our ice cream and joking with us. They were special needs young adults, one was the daughter of the owner. As we sat outside at a picnic table in the shade, the owner of the shop joined us for a friendly chat about our motorcycles.

We meandered on another 50 miles, lost another hour crossing back into Central Time. We still got to our hotel, the Spirit Lake Casino and Resort, in good time for the distance, arriving in the early evening. Jackie has us staying at another casino, but in her defense, in our original plans for the trip we would have been coming here to Spirit Lake Casino after having spent two weeks in Canada and Alaska. This would have been our first gambling excursion of the trip.

It's been an exulting kind of day, from the herds of cattle to the desolate prairies, to the corn fields, oil fields, harvested wheat fields, plus the jubilance of Salem Sue, the sunflower fields, making way for the elation of finding gas, celebrating it with ice cream. Our adventuresome spirit entices us to go downstairs for a little frolicsome gambling.

7-27-21 Field of Sunflowers

7-27-21. Cow at New Salem

7-27-21. Desolate country South Dakota

JULY 28ᵗʰ, 2021
Devil's Lake and Spirit Lake, North Dakota
12 miles

Today we rested for the most part. After yesterday's adventures it was time to reflect and rest. We had been planning to spend the day riding around Devils Lake, about 54 miles and tour the general area. But the weather was not enticing us to do anything, cool with heavy clouds, misty with rain expected in the afternoon. Jackie was fighting a head cold and didn't feel well. We made the decision to ride six miles into the town of Devils Lake for breakfast, car wash and a drug store stop.

Yesterday we drove through a swarm of crane flies, also known as mosquito hawks, even though they are mostly legs and wings, they are completely harmless. With their long gangly legs and sloppy flight patterns they tend to get stuck in all kinds of things, they made an awful mess smeared all over our bikes. We went into a car wash where I donned rubber gloves to remove the flies and grasshoppers out of the scoop-like vents on the front of my bike. Then with lots of soap and water, spray and rinse, lots of tender care, my bike turned out shimmering and sparkling, even in the dull, overcast, thick clouds, with temperatures in the low 70's.

We went to Mr. & Mrs. J's restaurant for the first coffee of the day and breakfast. I had an onion, mushroom skillet omelette and a big bowl of fruit. Jackie had her oatmeal with brown sugar. We found a drug store nearby to refortify our medication supply. The mist and imminent rain, were not conducive to doing any further exploration, so we drove back to the hotel after having traveled a total of 12 miles for the day.

Back in the hotel Jackie took a nap and I went to the casino to try to recoup some of my earlier loses, but it was a futile effort. Casinos were not my high point of this trip; they were more loser ability. After her rest Jackie came down feeling better, to join me for dinner at The View, the highlight of the day. Located on the third floor of the hotel, it overlooks sprawling Devils Lake and the marina just below. It would have been a stupendous view had it not been misty and cloud covered, but the atmosphere was still peaceful, fully inviting. The special for today was a New York strip steak, for $5 if you ordered an alcoholic drink. With roasted red skins and scalloped corn, my steak was scrumptious, with a nice glass of red wine to leisurely enjoy.

After the red wine it was my turn for a nap while Jackie went to play poker. After my nap it was time for ice cream. The weather had finally cleared, the sun was out. We walked to a nearby party store, got our supply of water for tomorrow and some goodnight snacks. I have checked and rechecked the weather heading across North Dakota, into Minnesota for tomorrow. It looks like we should stay dry. We realize now that we are on the homeward run. Heading home is kind of surreal as we have seen and experienced so much. In a few days this will all become a memory. One day at a time though, one day at a time in order to get home safely.

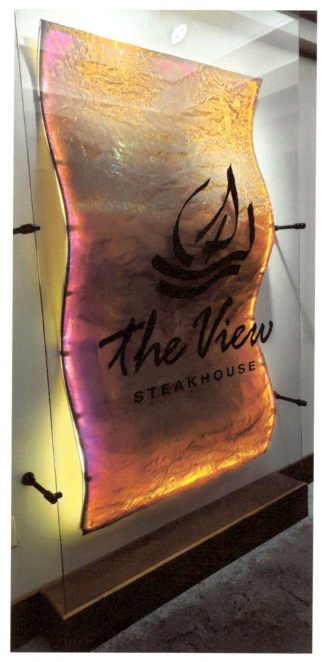

7-28-2021 Restaurant in Spirit Lake Casino & Resort.

JULY 29, 2021
Devil's Lake, South Dakota to Duluth, Minnesota
368 miles

We left the Devils Lake area about 9:30am, heading east on US-2, a two-lane highway with good shoulders all the way. With light traffic for the first 90 miles to Grand Forks, we enjoyed the easy flow of the rolling wheat, soybean and corn fields with the scenic blue of fishing lakes between.

As we were approaching Minnesota we passed the Air Force Base at Grand Forks, home of remotely piloted aircraft and training center. We also noticed a haze in the air that was not fog but it was blocking the sunlight. There was no smell so we did not realize at first that it was smoke. In Grand Forks we stopped to check the weather app, the red bar across the top of the screen warned of poor air quality due to the smoke from the fires blowing down out of Manitoba, Canada.

Smoke is made up of a mixture of gasses, fine particles, produced when wood and other organic materials burn. The biggest health threat is microscopic particles that can penetrate deep into our lungs. As we traveled east the smoke became denser. I estimated our visibility to be between one half and one mile at the most. The sun was bright filtering through the smoke but it had an odd aura.

My eyes began to water because of the ash in the air. My glasses turn dark plus I have a dark half-shield on the helmet, but it wasn't enough for my eyes. I had to add a pair of clip sunglasses to the mix so that I could see comfortably. The smell of smoke was almost non-existent; therefore I did not realize how dangerous it was.

Smoke continued as we watched the landscape change from fertile farmland, rolling plains, hill sides and rivers to mostly lakes, the Headwaters of the Mississippi river. Northern Minnesota is known as the land of 10,000 lakes.

The first city on the Headwaters of the Mississippi River is Bemidji, defined by its north-woods beauty, with its charms of Ojibwe heritage and artistic spirit, sits at the edge of both Lake Bemidji and Lake Irving.

We stopped here for gas and the need for ice cream. We were directed to the heart of Bemidji, the Big River Scoops. The slogan said "satisfy your hunger with mouth-watering ice cream". Since our nose and eyes were watering from the smoke, we thought that super premium ice cream would help correct the problem. Jackie had 5 mini scoops of their rich, delicious chocolate ice cream and I stuck with my large single peach yogurt. Jackie bought a bright pink t-shirt that verified the truth of our daily endeavor on our trip, it said it all, "Eat Ice Cream for Daily Happiness". While we were enjoying the relief of being smoke free eating our ice cream in Scoops, we looked out across the way to the blue waters of the lakefront. The statues of Paul Bunyan in his red checkered plaid shirt at 18 feet tall, and his trusty side-kick Babes the blue ox at 10 feet tall, were looking back at us. Together they have been welcoming tourists like us since 1937. It is said that Paul Bunyan was a super-sized logger who created Minnesota lakes when his boot prints filled with water, and dug Lake Superior as a watering trough for his giant blue ox.

Back into the smoke we continued our ride east, entering the serenity of the big lakes and big pines of the Chippewa National Forest. The forest boundary encompasses about 1.6 million acres and 1300 lakes. We rode for miles and miles and never saw a house. Modest homes, small casinos appeared once we entered the Leech Lake Indian Reservation. We were driving along peacefully on US 2 when suddenly a fish appeared. Is this a mirage in the smoke? A fish out of water is a strange sight. We were intrigued with the friendly fish, a 65-foot long, 15-foot wide, wooden structure in the shape of a Muskie, smiling at us with teeth the size of cedar posts. Jackie was excited for her son's Tom and Tim, both sport fisherman. She took her bike right up to the fish's open mouth and said "Hi", for a picture to send to them. The fish was originally built in the late 1950's as a drive-through restaurant, but people were a little queasy about food cooked in the fish. They were going next door to Louie's to eat. Now Louie's is "The Big Fish Supper Club" and the fish is the ambient welcome.

We continued for another hour surrounded by the peaceful blue lakes and pine forests, still breathing smoke. It wasn't until we reached the charming town of Grand Rapids, Minnesota, that our outdoor adventure of smoke-filled skies finally lifted. We rode in smoke without a mask for 182 miles, between Grand Forks North Dakota, and just after Grand Rapids, Minnesota. I had both a bandana and face mask in my trunk, so why did I not protect myself from all that smoke? Maybe it was the "cool" factor of not wearing a mask as a bike rider. Or maybe it was that the smell of smoke was so light that I had no sense of the danger of the fine particles inside it? It was a mistake I made that I would have to pay for in a few days.

The mix of lakes, forests and farm land continued all the way to Duluth. We fully celebrated the fresh air coming into our lungs for those last 80 miles.

Overwhelmed when we have to breathe polluted air, whether from fires or smog from within the cities, we take for granted the fresh air around us. We arrived at our LaQuinta Wyndham hotel on the north side of Duluth about 6:30pm, one more safe day down. Two more days to go to get home. This month is ending all too fast.

7-29-21 Big River Scoops

7-29-21. Jackie and the big fish.

7-29-21. The Big Fish

JULY 30, 2021
Duluth, Minnesota to Manistique, Michigan
362 miles

To end is much more difficult than to begin. When we began our trip, the future ran out before us, like an exciting adventure into the unknown, the miles ahead of us holding all kinds of possibilities. Now that we have come to the end, time has shortened. 700 miles from home this morning, things are beginning to look familiar. There is sadness and elation all at the same time.

Today is cool, jeans and a jacket, 72 degrees forecast for the high of the day, longing for shade is behind us. Within ten minutes of leaving the hotel, riding through the City of Duluth, we came around a curve in five lanes of traffic and the road began to slope downward. We suddenly have the welcoming view of Lake Superior, the harbors, two matching bridges, and the City of Superior, Wisconsin. Because of its average temperature of 40 degrees, Lake Superior is very clean. The cleanness shows in the color of the welcoming blue, deep, endless blue, stretching for 350 miles long and 160 miles wide, it is the largest and wildest of the Great Lakes.

We rode along US-2 from Duluth, Minnesota across the northern most part of Wisconsin, crossing through the Chequamegon-Nicolet National Forest. We rode through uplands, wetlands, rivers, streams, pine savannas, meadows and glacial lakes. We met aspen, maple, birch, beach, oak, basswood, ash, pine, spruce, fir and tamarack, trees and trees and more trees, with the sun shining through. This National Forest is comprised of 1.5 million acres of wilderness, bogs, wetlands and deep woods of every kind of tree, much of which was heavily logged in the early 20th century. During the 1930's the Forest was replanted with pine savannas to help restore the Ecosystem.

After the National Forest we entered the Bad River Indian Reservation, comprised of 124,200 acres, including wetlands and 500 miles of streams and rivers. 90% of the Reservation is wetlands, kept in a natural state where ever possible by the tribe. We observed the modest homes of The Lake Superior Tribe of Chippewa Indians, or Bad River Tribe for short. They sustain life by harvesting wild rice every August, grown plentiful in the 16,000 acres of high-quality wetlands, called Wisconsin's Everglades.

We crossed into home territory of the familiar state of Michigan, after having traveled through 18 other states over 30 days. Entering Michigan gave us a feeling of safety and comfort as we crossed the state line at Ironwood on US-2, rode through the Ottawa National Forest, a vast wilderness of a million-acre tract. We stopped at a roadside park for lunch, with the sun shining through the trees, enjoying the peaceful isolation. Everything is big here, rolling hills with dense forests, more than 500 lakes, and 2000 miles of streams and rivers, from the dramatic rocky shores of Lake Superior all the way across the Upper Peninsula to the shores of Lake Michigan.

This afternoon at Escanaba, within 360 miles of my home, I knew we were nearing Lake Michigan because I felt that temperature drop. Being from Michigan, we just know that within 10 miles of the shore of any of the Great Lakes, the temperature will drop significantly. Lake Michigan is the third largest of the five Great Lakes of North America, the only one lying wholly within the United States. Lake Michigan's name is derived from the Ojibwa word meaning "large lake". It is 118 miles wide and 370 miles long. In comparison to the cleanliness of Lake Superior, it is the most polluted of the Great Lakes. In 2018 nearly 22 million pounds of plastic were dumped into the Great Lakes – over half of which went into Lake Michigan.

We arrived at the Econo Lodge Lakeshore in Manistique in the cool late afternoon, thankful for having traveled through the tall, deep, glorious green forests, air free and fresh all day. Yesterday's adventure with the smoke from the forest fires had become a bad dream, except now the microscopic particles and ash have made a home in my lungs. All I want to do is sleep. The weather for tomorrow's travel back across the Mackinac Bridge and home is not looking good. We have brought our rain gear inside tonight, expecting to start out with it on in the morning. Tomorrow could turn out to be the coldest, rainiest day that we will have on the whole trip.

7-30-21. Lunch in the Ottawa National Park, UP of Michigan.

JULY 31, 2021
Manistique to Lapeer, Michigan
331 miles

This morning we woke up to rain. This should be the day for bells and whistles, our last day of this magnificent trip. But instead, it is raining to celebrate our ending. The only day of rain in the whole 8000 miles. So, we delayed leaving for about an hour, hoping it would quit. Watching the radar, we were hoping the weather would clear before we had to cross the Mackinac Bridge, 88 miles to the east. It is a five-mile-long suspension bridge, clearing 155 feet above the Straits of Mackinac, and 552 feet at its highest point. Dividing Lake Michigan from Lake Huron, the Mackinac Bridge suspends between St. Ignace on the Upper Peninsula and Mackinaw City on the Lower Peninsula. Crossing it on a bright sunny day, with no wind, on a motorcycle is a joy to behold, but with the cool wind and blowing rain, it becomes downright dangerous.

When we loaded our bikes, the sky was dark with low rain clouds and mist. We noticed police, fire and ambulances rushing by, going our way east on US2, with sirens blaring. While we stopped for breakfast a mile up the road, two ambulances came back by with lights and sirens. An hour later we drove past the remains of a traffic accident, the vehicles still in place, where police officers were measuring, photographing the scene. Amazingly, it was the first accident scene on the whole trip, coming home on our last day.

As we traveled east on US2 the traffic was heavy but flowing smoothly because of the many passing lanes along the route. Within two miles of the accident, we saw the reason when some fool dangerously passed us and several other vehicles a mile before one of the many passing lanes. There were several overhead flashing signs across the 88 miles, warning of delays to cross the Mackinac Bridge. We took our time riding in mist, squalls of light rain and at times, no rain, traveling through dense forests enclosed with swamps, lakes on both sides of us. The last 40 miles we traveled beside the familiar blue choppy waves of Lake Michigan.

We were apprehensive approaching the Mackinac Bridge because we anticipated the long wait in the mist and the rain. But we were surprised and elated. It had rained there but had now stopped, the pavement was dry. Like a higher being was looking after us, there was no wait, the traffic moved slowly and steadily, like a parade, across the Bridge. No spitting up of road water in our faces, no wind to rock the bikes. We rode across those five miles of bridge, excited to make the last big step to homecoming. To celebrate coming home, we stopped in Mackinac City at Devon's Fudge Shop. The fudge was not for Jackie or for me, but a present for Jackie's Mom, to salute her coming home.

As we got on I-75 southbound the familiar scenery of rolling hills and forests seemed to surround us. We felt comfortable here. I have driven this route countless times on countless daily trips. The traffic was light but the rain squalls started marching through, intermittently. Gaylord was home territory for my bike. Nine months ago, I found her sitting dust covered in the entrance at Extreme Sports, waiting for me. Imagine how far we have come together since then, 11,000 miles of adventure. She is like a trusted friend, if only she could talk, but Jackie makes up for some of the chatter.

Nothing like a friend to have us in mind, just when the heavy traffic picked up, we were into a stop and go pattern, my friend Smitty called to remind us of the usual backup around Bay City on I-75. Thankfully we decided to change our route, the traffic slowed, backed up twice more, so we got off I-75 at Frederic, took a familiar route across northeast lower Michigan to Standish.

We drove down North Old 27 into Grayling, east on M-72. Surprisingly we didn't meet a single vehicle on either road, except in Grayling. This route took us through the gracious tranquility of the half million acres of the Huron National Forest, vast acres of pine forests, wetlands, four large rivers, and trails open to the public for year-round recreation. It felt hospitable and comfortable to be back in my home territory of Michigan, the familiar smell of coming home, finding pleasure in the flowers, farmland and deep green forests.

We were ready to celebrate our arriving home with a Thanksgiving dinner at the Turkey Roost. We turned onto M-33 at Mio, came south down to Alger, then east on M-76 into Standish. From there we drove south on M-23 until we saw the welcome pink building of the Turkey Roost at Kawkawlin. It serves only turkey and the sides that go with turkey. No burgers, chicken, steak or fish. Just turkey. So, we had turkey with stuffing, mashed potatoes, gravy, corn, cranberry relish, coleslaw, biscuit and honey, all served in record time. Not to forget about the Strawberry Shortcake and whipped cream for dessert, as icing on the cake of our 8,00-mile trip.

As we left Kawkawlin we were able to pack up the rain gear, absorb the first sun of the day as we rode our last hour home. We turned onto M-13 from 23, rode through Bay City, across the Truman Bridge, south on M-15 through Vassar, further into Millington to the familiarity of Millington Rd. I waved good-bye to Jackie as I turned off and she continued on to Lapeer. That wave marked the end of our month-long trip, 7903 miles for me. If I had not done 170 miles on a flatbed, I too would have cleared 8000 miles like Jackie did. My average gas mileage was 34.3 miles per gallon, my average speed was 51miles per hour. I will not say what my maximum speed was, but one of us hit 100mph at one point going up through Nevada. The other rider hit 96mph.

7-31-21. Mackinac Bridge, Michigan

Conclusion

There is always an unknotting after having traveled for 31 days, day after day, for 8,000 miles. It is like I become part of the bike and the miles as they flow beneath me. Part of me could have ridden another 500 miles tomorrow, and on and on. As I soap up the bike and rinse off the suds, the road grime falls away with water from the hose. I towel it dry. I too am awash with the finality of the end. As I settle the bike back home, in her familiar spot in the garage, I let the miles go.

I unload my orange bag with all kinds of presents: a vase from the Hood Canal and another from Yellowstone, shirts from Sturgis, sweatshirts from California and Michigan, H-D gloves, magnets from everywhere for the refrigerator, video from the Grand Canyon Imax, cups & coffee from Portland, a sandstone souvenir from the Continental Divide, a shell from the Pacific Ocean, pajama pants and a bracelet from Yellowstone, cups from Mt. Rushmore for the Liley's, a golf ball from Las Vegas. We celebrated all these memories strewn around us. All these places have come home to us, all these moments, all these miles.

The ashes from the forest fires, driving through 182 miles of smoke across northern Minnesota without a mask, is playing havoc with my lungs. They will take a little longer to heal, needing two rounds of antibiotics over the next ten days, and lots of sleep before I am finally well. The final residue of the global crisis hitting home. Ironically, it is the smell of everything that stays with me. With my lungs damaged from smelling smoke too liberally, I remember and celebrate, the daily wonder of breathing in so much deliciousness and exhilaration, as we traveled day by day. A motorcycle is a vehicle to continually absorb, and then let go, the smells that assail us. From the beginning we were like a couple of kids, rejoicing in our new adventure. The corn in Illinois was already head high and I could smell its sweet scent. The old man on his porch in Missouri, is a friendly memory, watering a garden of surrounding pots filled with petunias, sweet peas, alyssum, moonflower on the railing, on the steps and the floor of the porch itself. We called out to him complimenting on their exhilarating smell. We continued riding, surrounded by the scent of freshly mowed grass repeated in every town.

Out amongst the open fields the luscious smells of fresh cut hay, tangy and earthy, greeted us day after day as we traveled. Dairy farms have a smell all of their own, combined aroma of milk and manure. Fresh, white, clean, fruity nuance of milk mixed with the offal of cows makes for a fascinating but distinct odor. Sometimes farms in Idaho were watering and I could smell the silage scent of wet corn stalks, along with cows standing, steaming, soaking up the wet pastures.

For the whole trip we found it agreeable but lamentable, as we traveled day after day, the countryside has its own smell of decay, with the decomposing bodies of dead animals littering the roadside. A little less pungent but just as obnoxious is the occasional smell of tobacco and marijuana emitting from passing vehicles or on the streets in the cities. The smell of diesel exhaust swirled around us as we slowed down in the cities, and the odor of gasoline, made up of 150 chemicals, intoxicating to some and offensive to others. We got so used to it, we hardly smelled it at all.

We got accustomed to the smell of gasoline surrounding us, but it was nothing compared to the odor of sulfur, reminiscent of burnt matches, skunk and rotted eggs in Yellowstone National Park. The heat, oozing mud with steam wafting from the holes, was a vapor cloud of stink. Satan would smell like that. How can something surrounded by stunningly beautiful views, smell so abundantly bad. The American bison, a symbol of the United States, that we encountered in Yellowstone and Needles parks, is a close comparison in smell to the obnoxiousness of sulfur. He carries with him his own mangy, unwashed scent, partly caused by rolling in his own dusty wallow as he is urinating, spreading his

scent around for all to smell. As I was awed by his shaggy fearlessness, the strength of his smell was a bouquet of rankness.

The wild burro has a welcome smell, just in the way he gave up the only tree for shade in Beaty, Nevada, a brown desert town. With all of his friends and family he gave us his shade. He was such a friendly fellow, I just wanted to pet him. How do I remember the smell of shade, given up by a band of burros, other than welcome? The brown fur of the burros blended in with the brown tumbleweeds tumbling over and over in the surrounding desert, just parched dust and dirt, with no obvious smell at all, other than the friendliness of feeling sheltered.

Feeling sheltered was what we felt when we arrived at the blue of the Pacific Ocean. After several days of tolerating the smell of brown heat of the desert, the smell of ash from forest fires, the wet renewal of the ocean is enticing to my toes. To my nose it is inviting with its slightly briny scent of salty, fishy ocean air, swirling my senses. The towering heights and majestic serenity of the Redwoods is a perfect companion to the Pacific Ocean and its flavor. Ever to remember, the salt sand smell of the ocean mixed into the woodsy dirt smell of the Redwoods is an enticing cocktail for my senses to process. The acute scent of redwood mixed with the overwhelming odor of dirt, enveloped me. This was not a musty smell, just a fascinating odor, a mild spice with earthy undertones and a tinge of sweetness, that I can still smell.

But it was shade that became the fulcrum of our trip, our search for shade. The smell of it varied with enjoyment and relief, according to the source of that shade. The sun has a smell all of its own, it seems to take over and enhances the smell and substance of whatever it absorbs into its radiant heat. Riding in 114 degrees heat had a way of melting down our senses so that everything we touched and smelled we were afraid of. In Wittman, Arizona sitting on my running board for a bit of shade, close to fainting, I realized the sun could kill us in short order. But the shade was our savior, not that day with a spindly little tree with its small patch of shade in a church yard in Wittman, but the forests that celebrated the shade and the smell of it for nearly half of our trip. The deep national pine forests smelling of a pleasantly mild, musty, turpentine scent, all along CA299 in northern California for 150 miles, to Whidbey Island in Washington with its Douglas firs and western hemlock trees. The clean, woodsy, piney smell of Yellowstone National Park, the dense forests of the Needles Parks in South Dakota gave us needed relief. Along US2 through Minnesota, Wisconsin and the Upper Peninsula of Michigan the forests gave off an earthy, reassuring smell from the bark, moss and wood oils of the aspen, maple, birch, oak, basswood, ash, pine, and many more. The National Forests with their millions and millions of acres of trees, almost every species, shading our way.

CPSIA information can be obtained
at www.ICGtesting.com
Printed in the USA
BVHW021514200922
647488BV00002B/24